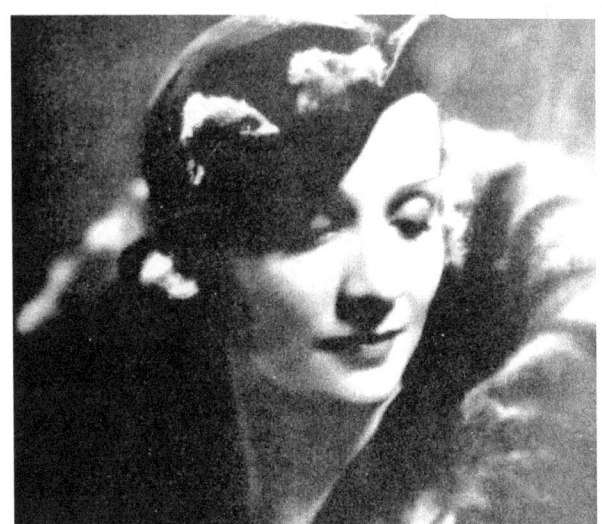

MARLENE

DIETRICH

THE MOVIE GUIDE

By Chris Wade

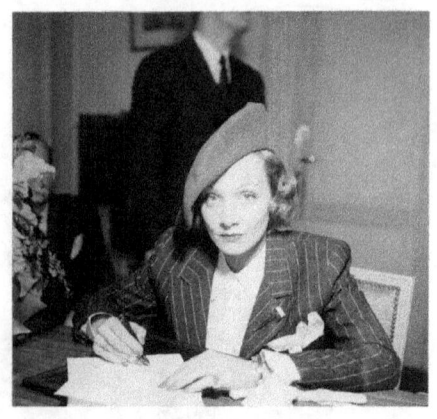

MARLENE DIETRICH: THE MOVIE GUIDE

by Chris Wade

Wisdom Twins Books, 2019

wisdomtwinsbooks.weebly.com

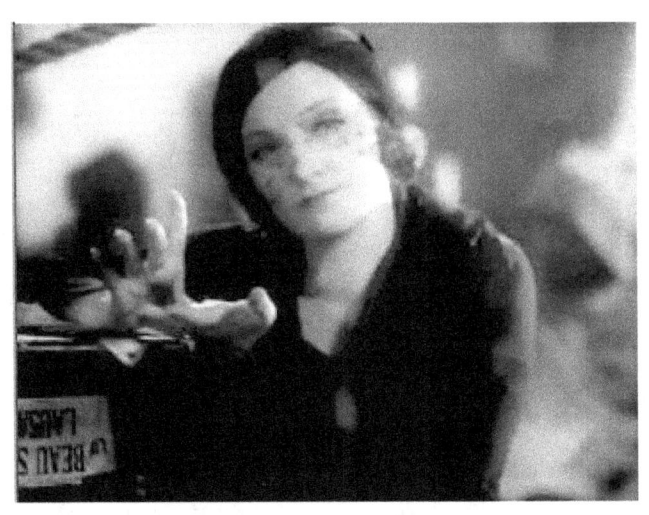

MARLENE

DIETRICH

THE MOVIE GUIDE

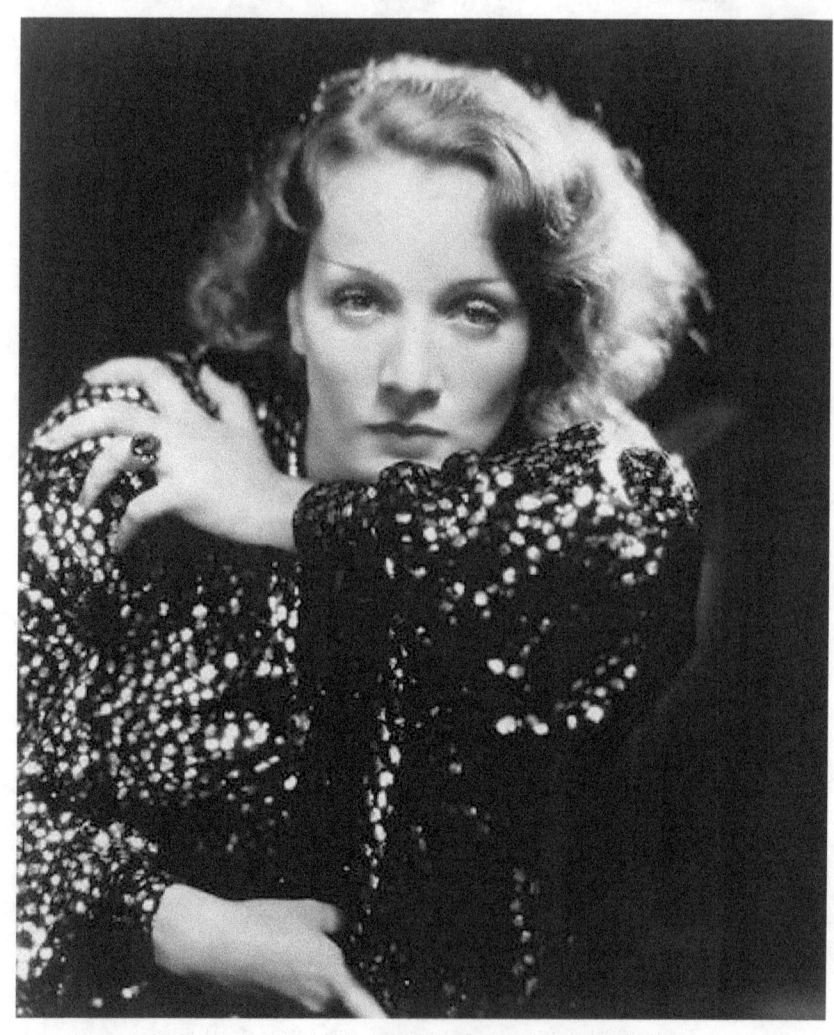

CONTENTS

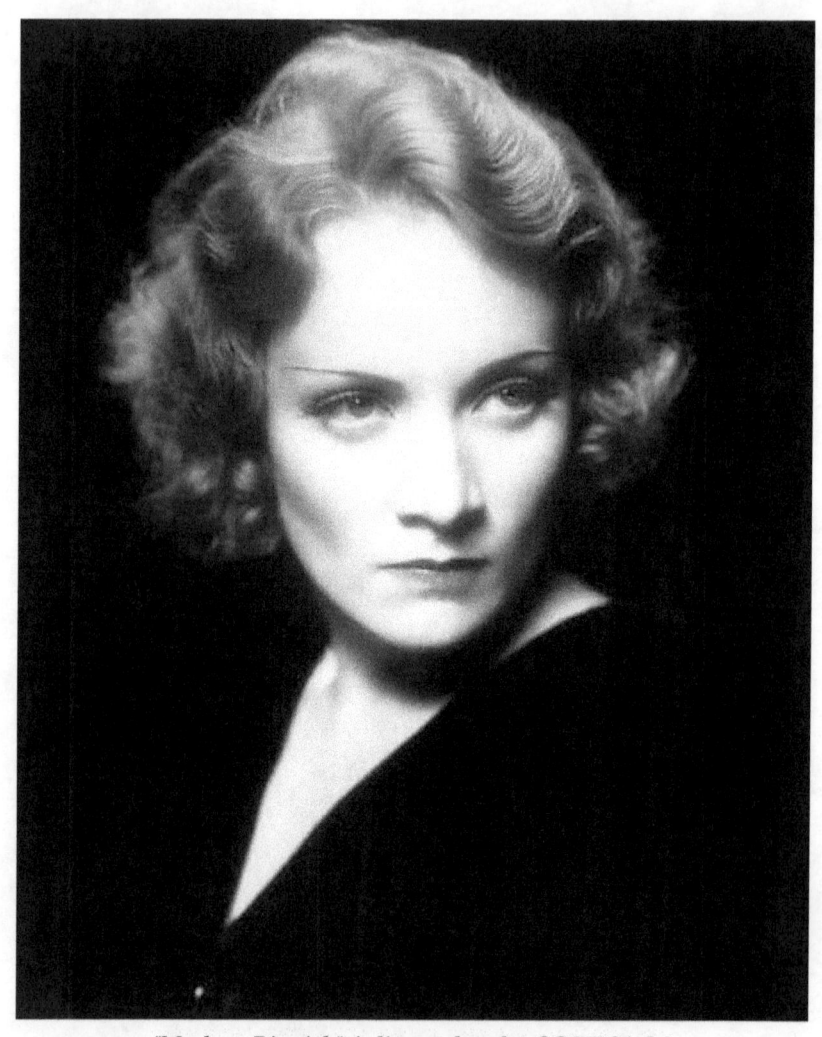

"Marlene Dietrich" is licensed under CC BY-SA 2.0

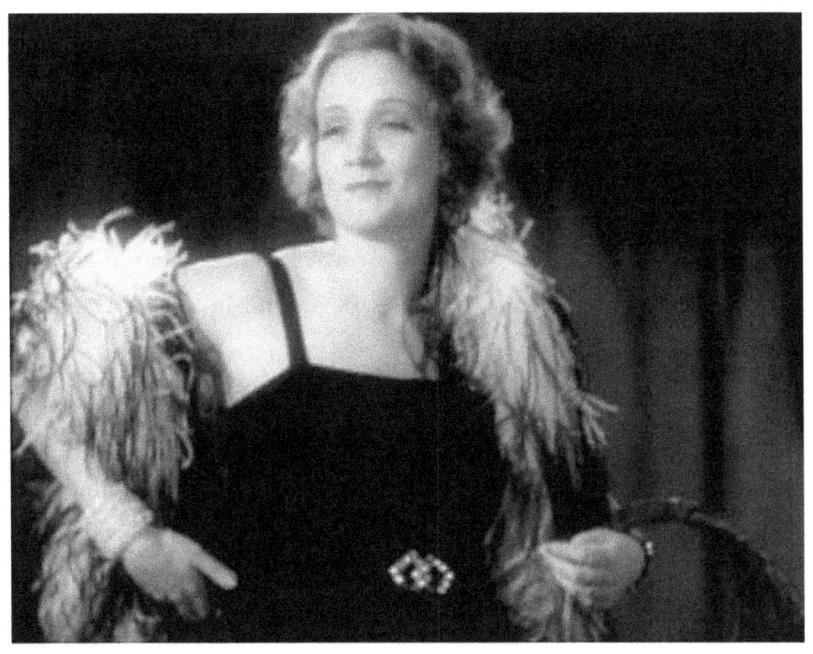

INTRODUCTION

When exploring the film career of Marlene Dietrich, and her roles within them, one is not accessing performances of extreme complexity, of subtle nuances and developments in mood - at least not for the most part. One is simply enjoying heightened, stylised movie magic. Yes, Dietrich was a fabulous presence in the movies' golden era, but she was primarily a star of the screen in the truest sense (and stage of course), known for her glamour, larger than life exuberance and seductive appeal. Films were manufactured for her as idealised vehicles, and she became the central work of art in almost everyone one. We were there to bask in her glory, gaze at those famous legs and the exotic costumes. But she was also in some truly brilliant films, and her range in them, still admittedly within the tight Dietrich parameter, was more varied than you might think. In particular, her work with director Josef von Sternberg is still strong today, but even later into her career she was pushing herself, giving more complicated performances as she aged.

These days, awareness of Dietrich varies. Older generations may remember her from when she was still around in the latter part of her screen career, popping up in brief cameos, many nods to her illustrious past; films buffs will know her retrospectively from her work with von Sternberg, those classic movies from the early thirties; younger generations may know the name and face but nothing else; while some, regrettably, will be absolutely clueless all together. This is, of course, inevitable, for the passage of time naturally sees that world famous legends soon fade away into obscurity. But some stars of the past deserve to stay relevant, not just for the work they left behind, but for their importance and impact on culture. For me, Dietrich is one of them.

She was born Marie Magdalene Dietrich, nicknamed Lena by her family as she grew up in Rote Insel, Schonberg, now a district of Berlin. Dietrich had already become a fixture of Germany's stage in the late twenties before her fame. She began working professionally in her early twenties, firstly playing violin for an orchestra providing music for silent films, before taking up acting. Through the decade she appeared in silent films and in the theatre. She married Rudolf Sieber in 23 and they had a daughter, Maria, the following year.

Her first worldwide film hit, Josef von Sternberg's 1930 classic The Blue Angel, made her a worldwide fascination. Josef and Marlene delicately crafted an image of enigmatic sensuality, not just by careful lighting and costume, but also presentation. Think, for instance, of when she first appears in 1932's Blonde Venus, swimming naked in a lake, ogled by a group of men while she and her liberated friends frolic in the water. And who could forget the iconic moment in Shanghai Express, when she stands quietly, lit from above like a sensuous angel, smoking a cigarette with shaking hands. This picture, with Marlene as glowing goddess, has become one of the most enduring images of film's golden age.

Marlene captured the world's imagination through a deadly, enrapturing combination of factors, namely her glamour, her exotic classiness and her sex appeal. But Dietrich sensuality was not conveyed distastefully. Unlike today's female stars, who display their scantily clad bodies gratuitously just as present Hollywood requires, Marlene teased the audience, keeping herself at a certain distance but unveiling just enough of her mystique to hook the viewer from her first moment on the screen to the very last. Indeed, watching a Dietrich film is rather like being under a spell, and one cannot help but be seduced by the illusion created by both Dietrich and her director. As manufactured as her image may have been, one never gets the feeling of being tricked or duped; more hypnotised, won over. After Sternberg she was freed in some regards to explore wider roles and genres; comedies, thrillers and dramas, and she excelled in them all. Josef may have helped create the Dietrich image, but he also held her captive for a time.

This book is a guide to the films which are too often overlooked in favour of the image, the immortal sex symbol status. Dietrich is still remembered today and many see her as relevant. Her bisexuality and playful attitude towards sex itself has seen her become a gay icon.

Marlene was such a strong personality, such a star, that it's natural the films often came - and still come - second to the image. This book, the first on her filmography itself for many years, looks at her appearances from a modern viewpoint while also appreciating how extraordinary she was in her own era. From her first silent pictures, through the essential Sternberg films and her later movie appearances, it's the complete picture of a story and a development told out on screen in a variety of engaging performances and a large number of classic pictures. Other books, like Steven Bach's biography and her daughter Maria Riva's tell-all epic tome, give us Marlene the woman and her life and times. This volume examines the worth of the work that made her famous in the first place.

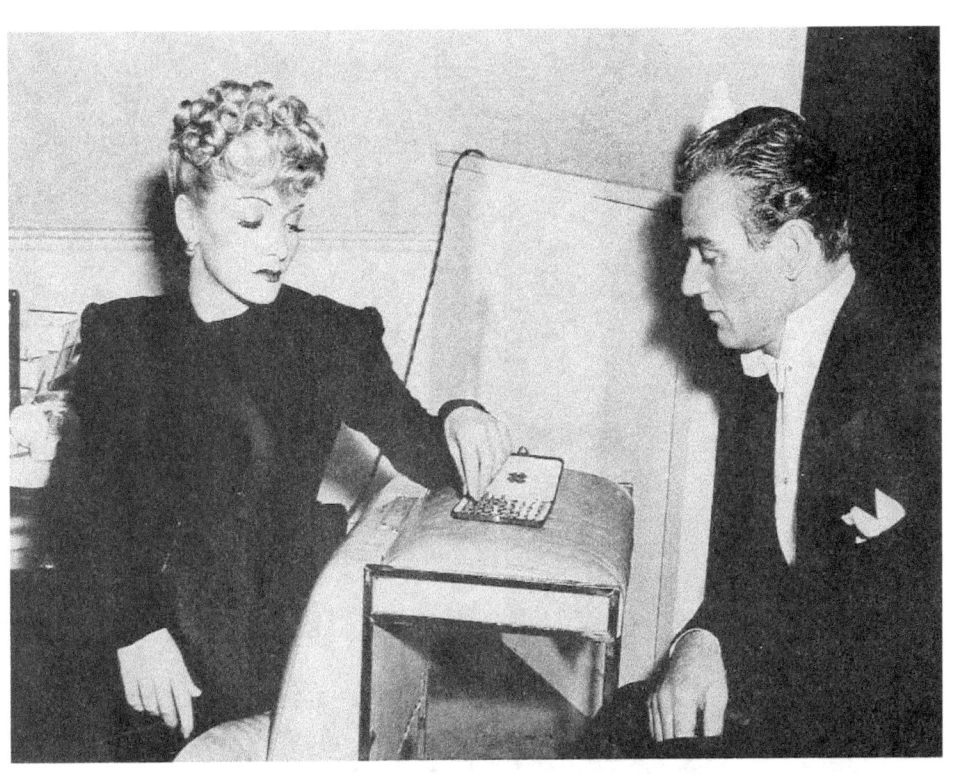

Dietrich plays chess with John Wayne, 1943

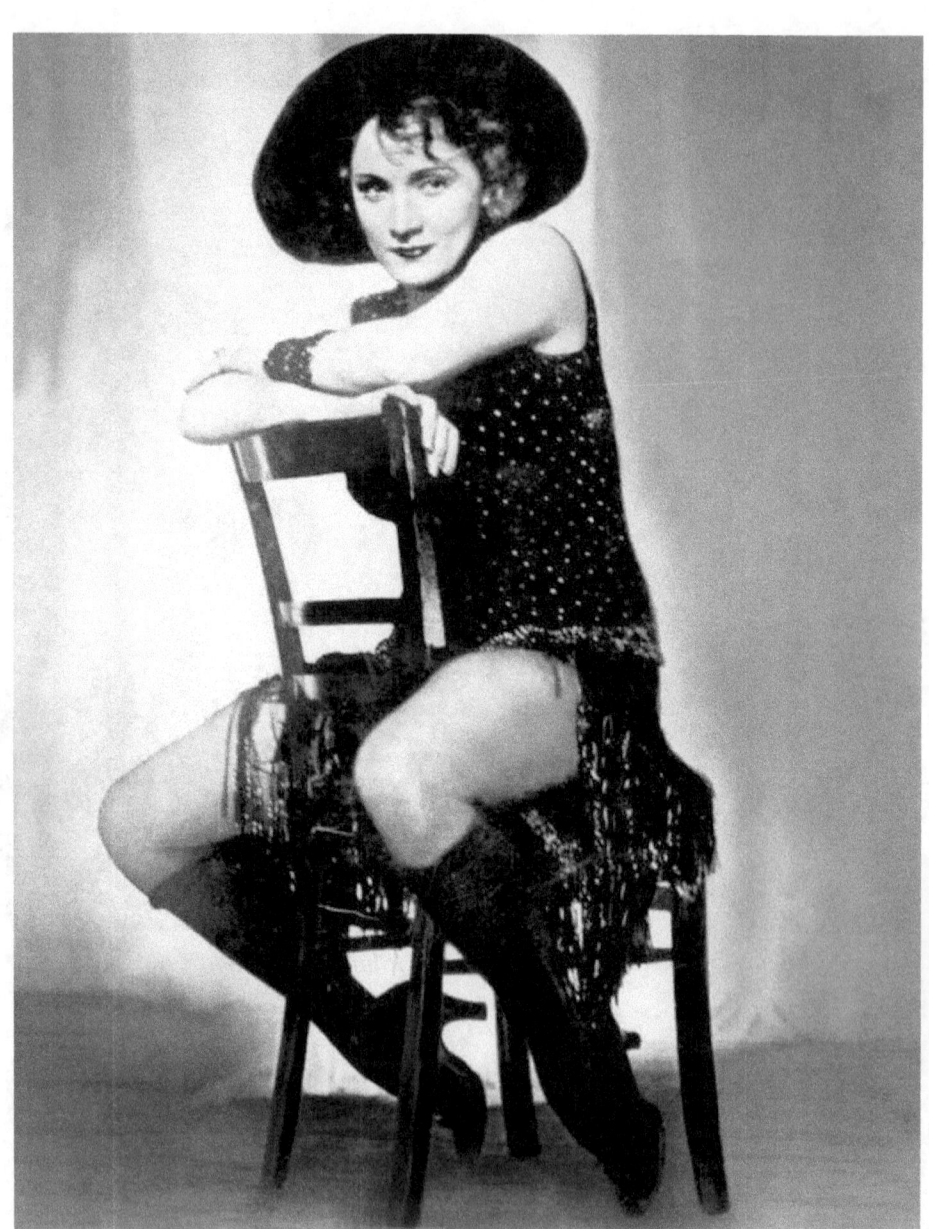

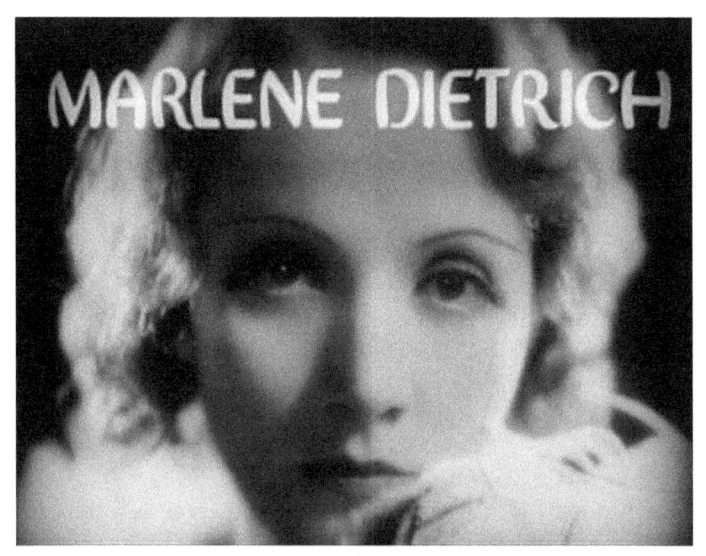

THE FILMS

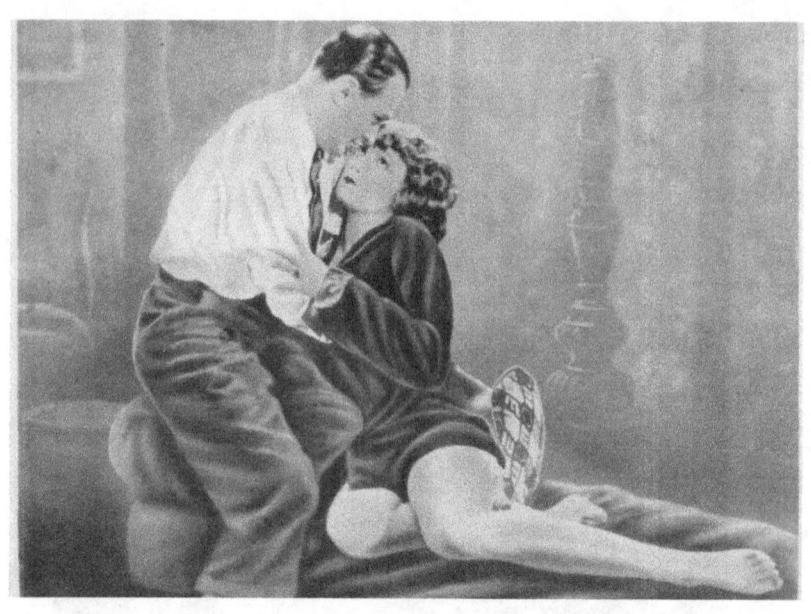

THE EARLY SILENT PICTURES (1923 - 1929)

The earliest part of Dietrich's on screen career is often forgotten these days, perhaps because people choose to believe that she exploded out of nowhere straight on to the screen in The Blue Angel, the role that made her a star. In reality, she had appeared in nearly twenty German silent films before Hollywood had even heard of her. Granted, in such crackly, often gothic surroundings she is not the Marlene Dietrich we know from the golden period of thirties Hollywood. The fact that most of these films are impossible to track down also means they harbour a mythical quality. Stills have emerged for some and Dietrich, indeed, often looks far from the queen of seduction of the thirties. But interestingly, as the silent films go on, she begins to morph into the glamorous icon of von Sternberg's fantasies, slowly edging towards the icon we know and love. In the silent movies we are lucky to be able to see, Marlene harbours true star power beneath her hesitance, albeit in its primitive form, and still commands the screen whenever she appears. The films that have survived, such as Cafe Elektric, are vital in the development of Dietrich's screen persona. In many ways, her performance in The Blue Angel is the kind an actor might have given in silent cinema, and it would take a picture or two for her to adapt to sound.

Her first movie role was in The Little Napoleon, where she received 12th billing. She filmed her part over the summer in 1922 for director Georg Jacoby, who had been impressed by her audition. She had a slightly larger role in Tragedy of Love with Emil Jannings, playing the part of Lucy for director Joe May. As the picture starred the then highly popular Jannings, the film was seen by many in Germany. Thankfully for Dietrich, she even managed to get a few close ups, such as her first phone scene and the one where she peeks through opera glasses. Until she did The Blue Angel, she considered this her favourite film part, though she was steadily employed in the theatre throughout the whole of the twenties.

In Many by the Wayside she worked for the first time with director William Dieterle, whom would film her twenty years later, and more memorably, in Kismet. Here she has a small role as a peasant girl, and it remains the only reason the film will ever be written about today, almost 100 years since it was filmed. She also worked for director Lothar Mendes in the mysterious The Monk from Santarem, of which very little is known, as well as 1924's Leap Into Life for Johannes Guter. In what sounds like a step backwards, she was an extra in 1925's Dancing Mad, appearing as a dancer. (She also appeared uncredited in Madame Wants No Children as a dancer.)

Manon Lescaut was a bigger chance for her to shine, though again it was a mere supporting turn as Michele. In 1927 she had a bigger role in A Modern Dubarry, working for Alexander Korda, who would be a vital figure in her future. She had only three scenes in this buried treasure, though she was famously billed as Marlaine Dietrich on the credits.

Also in 1927 she was in two films for director Willi Wolff, playing Sophie in the Imaginary Baron, and Edmee in Heads up Charley. These films are totally forgotten today and only remain of note, for the most part at least, for the billing of Dietrich, who was edging her way closer to The Blue Angel and the guidance of Josef von Sternberg. (Fact: the heirs of producer Ellen Richter promised to withhold release of the film in Dietrich's life time.)

She had a larger role in 1927's His Greatest Bluff, appearing as Yvette, though it was nothing to her first sizeable part in the Austrian silent mini classic, Cafe Elektric. Here she played Erni, daughter of a rich industrialist who starts a romance with a pickpocket. Cafe Elektric is the first time we see Dietrich as a possible star, a film which remains easy to view today. Directed by Gustav Ucicky, it's a genuinely enjoyable silent movie worthy of your time, Dietrich or not.

Dietrich as we came to know her in the thirties begins to look clearer and more recognisable in 1928's Princess Olala, playing the part of Chichotte de Gastone, and also in I Kiss Your Hand Madame, a picture which saw a US release in 1932 after Dietrich's Hollywood success kicked in, though she probably wasn't too pleased about it.

The next three films moved Marlene more towards her look in The Blue Angel, and she appeared confident and more assured about acting on screen. Already well versed on the stage, adapting herself to movie acting was a challenge. Her face, however, was clearly made for the camera, and her piercing eyes become magnetic in the silent settings, where there is no dialogue and emphasis remains on looks. In The Woman One Longs For, she was almost in Morocco territory, even smoking at one point and appearing very close indeed to thirties Dietrich. In 1929's The Ship of Lost Souls, she dazzled as Ethel in this moody thriller, and in her final film role before The Blue Angel, she starred as Evelyne in Dangers of the Engagement Period for director Fred Sauer. It was while working for Sauer that Dietrich was alternatively appearing on the stage in a show alongside Hans Albers, an engagement which led to The Blue Angel and her relocation to Hollywood, where von Sternerg would sharpen her image and turn her into the deadly Dietrich who captured the world's imagination.

No icon is born over night, even if it appears like they were. Behind her dynamic arrival on the world stage in The Blue Angel is a run of forgotten, crusty old movies, not to mention the stage work of which there remains no filmed footage. Dietrich's journey to being an icon and world renowned performer took a whole decade of slogging her way to the top. When her break did arrive however, Dietrich appeared fully formed, a natural, a woman born to be on the screen.

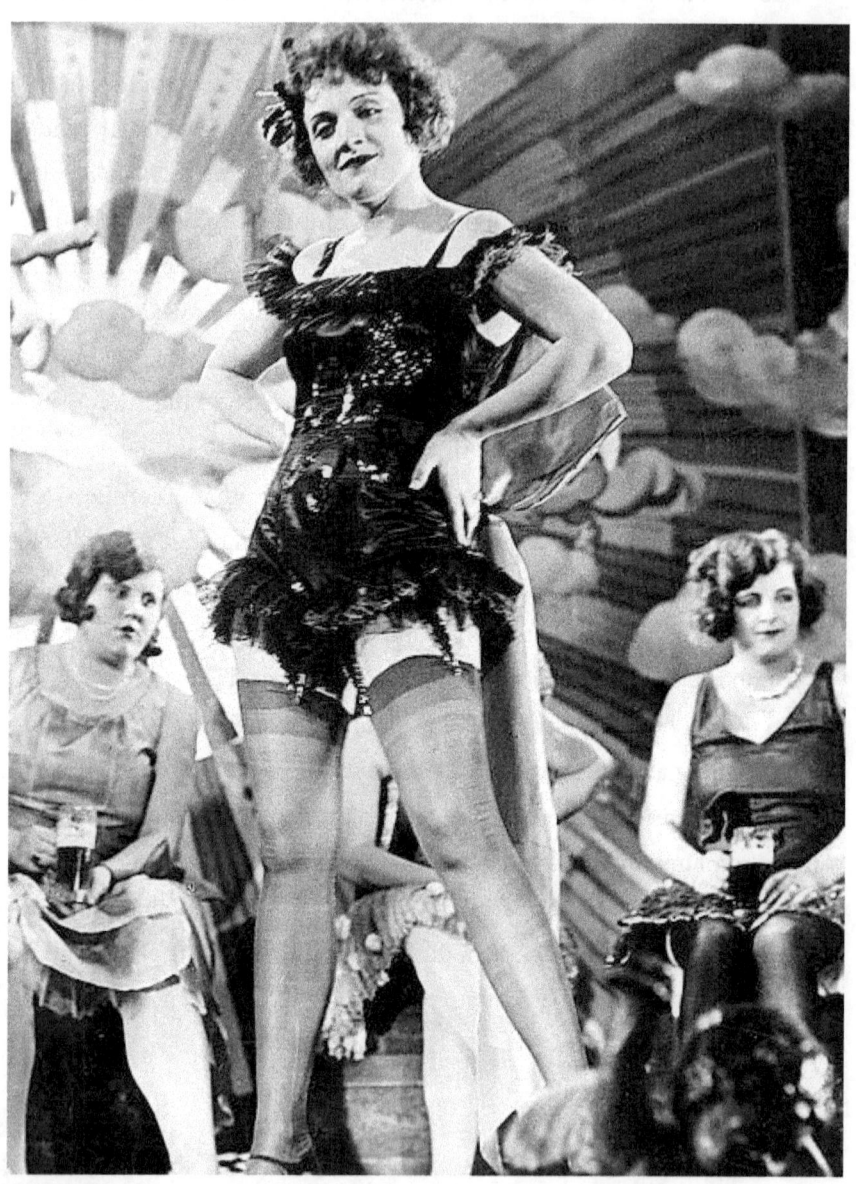

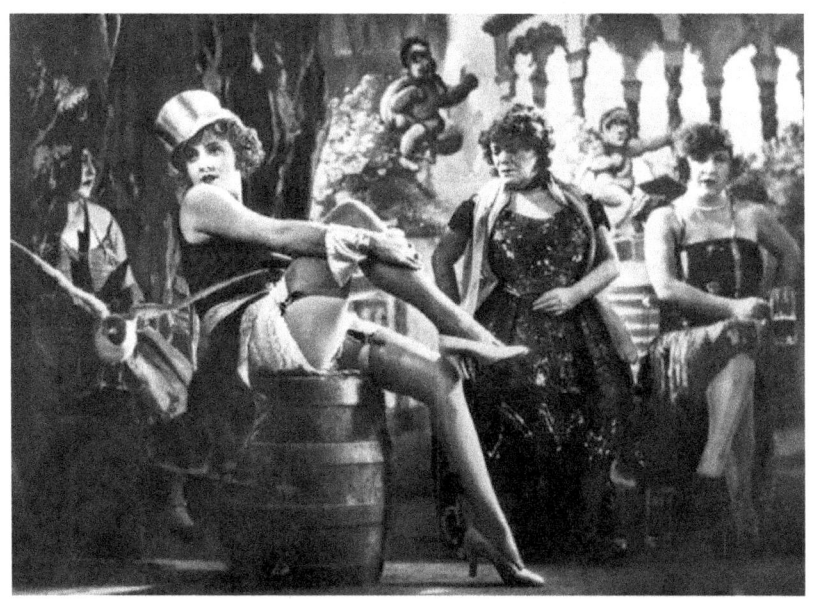

THE BLUE ANGEL (1930)

By 1929, Josef von Sternberg, the Austrian-American filmmaker, had directed a few successful movies for Paramount Pictures in the USA. Before establishing himself at the mammoth studio he'd had a colourful time in movie land, though not all of his film adventures were seen through to completion. First off, he'd had a brush with Mary Pickford, at one point Hollywood's most popular female star, but his proposed project for her was deemed too avant-garde, and after a stint at MGM, he was given the chance to direct Charlie Chaplin's A Woman of the Sea, a film which was destroyed after completion by Chaplin himself. Finally he found satisfaction, after a series of ill fated projects, in a run of films from 1928's The Last Command to 1929's The Case of Lena Smith. After he made 1929's Thunderbolt, he was approached by UFA, Germany's Paramount, to take on a film called The Blue Angel, to star Emil Jannings as Professor Immanuel Rath, an academic who suffers a tragic downfall when he becomes obsessed with a cabaret singer by the name of Lola-Lola.

Though it was to be a vehicle for Jennings, then at his height, the part of Lola-Lola was vital in von Sternberg's eyes, and for this part he needed to find the perfect actress, someone who could be sexy and appealing but do so without effort, without trying too hard to melt celluloid. When a young Marlene Dietrich auditioned, and in truth seemed half uninterested, von Sternberg saw in her the quality he had been searching for. Though no wide eyed innocent, she did look youthful and fresh. The director knew she was the only woman for the job, but the studio needed persuading, unsure that an unknown could carry such a film and convince in the central part.

Originally the part was going to go to Lucie Mannheim, a popular singer of the time, with both the studio and Jannings himself firm on this choice. Sternberg however found her unappealing, stating she did not have the necessary glamour to light up the screen. Other close calls were Brigitte Helm, who turned out to be busy, and Kathe Haack nearly signed, but any alternatives were binned when von Sternberg met Marlene and was bewitched by her peculiarity. When he met her in person for the first time he jumped in the air and shouted "It's Lola!" Haack was paid off and sent on her way, and Marlene, acting cool as a cucumber, took her place. In Josef's mind, Dietrich was vital for the film to succeed, and at one point told Heinrich Mann, the writer of the book the film was based on, that "the success of this film will be found in the naked thighs of Miss

Dietrich!'" Eventually he got his way and Dietrich was cast. Seeing her potential, von Sternberg began to mould her to his liking.

The Blue Angel was actually shot twice, once in German and again with the actors speaking in English. Though both edits are excellent, one could say the songs are best heard in English, if only to put across the sincerity for English speaking viewers, while the movie itself is best seen in German, where the actors are truer to their roles and more natural/comfortable with their performances. In either form, the film succeeds not because of its loose story, nor even in the addictive tension between the ageing cuckold and his manipulative object of obsession, but because of Marlene herself. From the moment she appears, we are transfixed. Dietrich is at her most pure, her most fresh, plucked from the German stage and put forth to the world. She may have been von Sternberg's icon, gazing down at he and Emil Jannings from her pedestal, as if they were one and the same man (and in many ways, it has to be said, they are), but the power was in her hands.

The movie was a success in America, its release held up until January of 1931 when her first fully English speaking role in Morocco was unveiled. Her rise to fame was sudden and unexpected. Overnight it seemed that Dietrich was a sensation. Jannings is also brilliant in his role, going from respected academic to shameful clown, his descent into bedlam masterfully handled. Yet it is completely Dietrich's show; and how could it not be, when all the drive of the plot and the poor man's downfall rests on her sexuality, her power and ability to turn a man into mush. She is the seductress, and he is mere putty in her hands.

That is not to say Dietrich/Lola-Lola's manipulative characteristics make her an unsavoury character. It is very much not the case, because despite her torturing of the older man, she still seems innocent, though clearly being far from it. Others have voiced this opinion too, in particular the film critic Michael Aubriant, who wrote in 1966, "We probably all were victims of an illusion... the Marlene we rediscover is candour personified; a good-hearted little trouper, a bit overly romantic, perhaps, flattered by the attention of a pedant old enough to be her papa, dragging him along for four years like a ball and chain. Not a trace of malice. She prefers this clod to her gilded coxcombs. Of course she ends up cuckolding him, but almost against her own will. The idiot dies from it. Good riddance!"

A lesser actress, perhaps someone trying too hard and pushing for sensuality on a more conventional scale, would have transformed Lola-Lola into a tyrant, a mean hearted she-devil using a love sick man as a toy, something to merely amuse her when she should fancy. But Dietrich handles it perfectly, torn between a flattery and genuine fondness and a carelessness which is impossible to avoid given the huge age difference and the way Jannings willingly degrades himself for her love. Though a guided performance led by the more experienced von Sternberg, Dietrich's naivety works in her favour. Some critics at the time claimed her acting skill to be so-so, but the flatness she harbours here makes the performance a successful one.

Another important point to make is that The Blue Angel, despite its sound, dialogue, music and legendary songs, is very much in its spirit a silent picture, though this may sound like a ludicrous contradiction when taken literally. The performances however have the purity of the best of silent film, when more is said in actions, especially the more subtle ones, than many of the actual lines. And Marlene handles herself as she had in her silent pictures, effortlessly gliding along, getting by on careful mannerisms and body language, suggestive behaviour and gestures. It's a tour de force of primal film performance, enhanced by the visual presentation rather than dialogue.

The visuals are all von Sternberg's, but the man himself admitted how much he relied on and needed Dietrich not just as a physical embodiment of his masochistic lusts, but as a collaborator with her own valid ideas. "I never had a better assistant than Miss Dietrich," he said as an older man, "if I wanted to sit down she brought me the chair. She did everything she could to understand me. She was very easy."

Dietrich herself recalled the collaboration on The Blue Angel with simplicity, suggesting that the analysis and theories about their masochistic relationship has perhaps been exaggerated down the years. "He just told me what I should do," she recalled later. "All directors do that but he was the very first director I had, so naturally I did exactly what he wanted."

Watching the film now, so aware of Dietrich's star power and strong persona in other films, The Blue Angel is an interesting document in regards to her development and moulding in the hands of her mentor. Clearly un-established, fresh faced and a little more filled out than the Dietrich of subsequent films, the roots of the icon are being planted and it is von Sternberg doing the watering. He saw in Marlene the very thing he was looking for, something that neither she nor the film studio could see for themselves. He was prophetic, but he was also vitally instrumental in ensuring that Dietrich fulfilling her potential.

The Blue Angel did set Marlene on the right path, but she was never that kind about it in her older years. She found Lola-Lola to be coarse, often diminished the film's reputation as an important landmark in cinema history and even said it was "enough to make you puke." One can understand why she would look down on her Hollywood debut, especially when you consider the more careful and calculated Dietrich of Shanghai Express and Morocco. In the later von Sternberg films and beyond, Marlene, though still guided by her directors, seems like a creation of her own, owned by herself and nobody else. She is powerful, assured and confident, whether embodying exoticism with effortless ease in Shanghai Express or fleeing conventions in her restless fugitive lifestyle in Blonde Venus. Here though, there is a virginal quality and it is evident that she is merely reflecting back the fantasies and masochistic perversions of von Sternberg.

Speaking in 1960 to The Observer, she made a reference to her image, the present one as an icon approaching sixty, and the one in the primitive Blue Angel, clearly seeing a distinction between the two. "The image? A conglomerate of all the parts I've ever played on the screen. When I was in The Blue Angel people thought that was me: they really thought that was me!"

Even now, almost ninety years after it was made, the film has a stark brutality to it, an emotionally cold bluntness which has not dimmed down the decades. It's as if we are to delight in Janning/Rath's suffering, revel in the perversity of his breakdown. The Los Angeles Times wrote in 1991 that "it *is* often hard to

24

stomach. Rath, a vulnerable but pedantic high school teacher, sinks way beyond his own protective self-righteousness after he encounters Lola-Lola. She's as immune to self-criticism as he is ruled by it. Lola-Lola is all impulse and sensuality; she's a sexual fantasy made real. This film can make you feel voyeuristic, especially by the queasy ending when Rath's ruin is complete. The famous rooster-crowing scene near the finale puts a man-gone-mad on display. The moment is emotionally over-inflated, but effective nonetheless."

There is a pointed, direct quality to The Blue Angel which was missing from the Dietrich/von Sternberg movies from here on. Marlene herself transformed too, from the knife voiced Lola-Lola to the more seductive, purring siren of Morocco and onwards, a slinkier and more graceful creature, more conscious too and well aware where the best lighting came from. But there is a freshness about Marlene in The Blue Angel which makes it exciting. Like watching Charlie Chaplin falling about in his early Keystone films, The Blue Angel gives the viewer an insight into the makings of a legend.

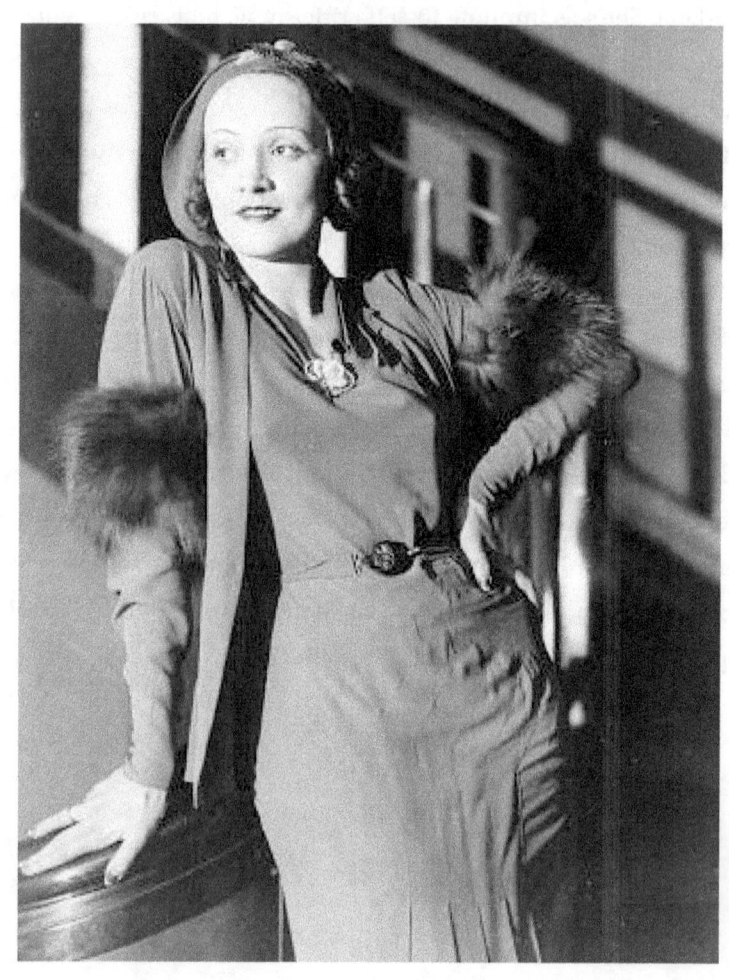

Dietrich in 1930

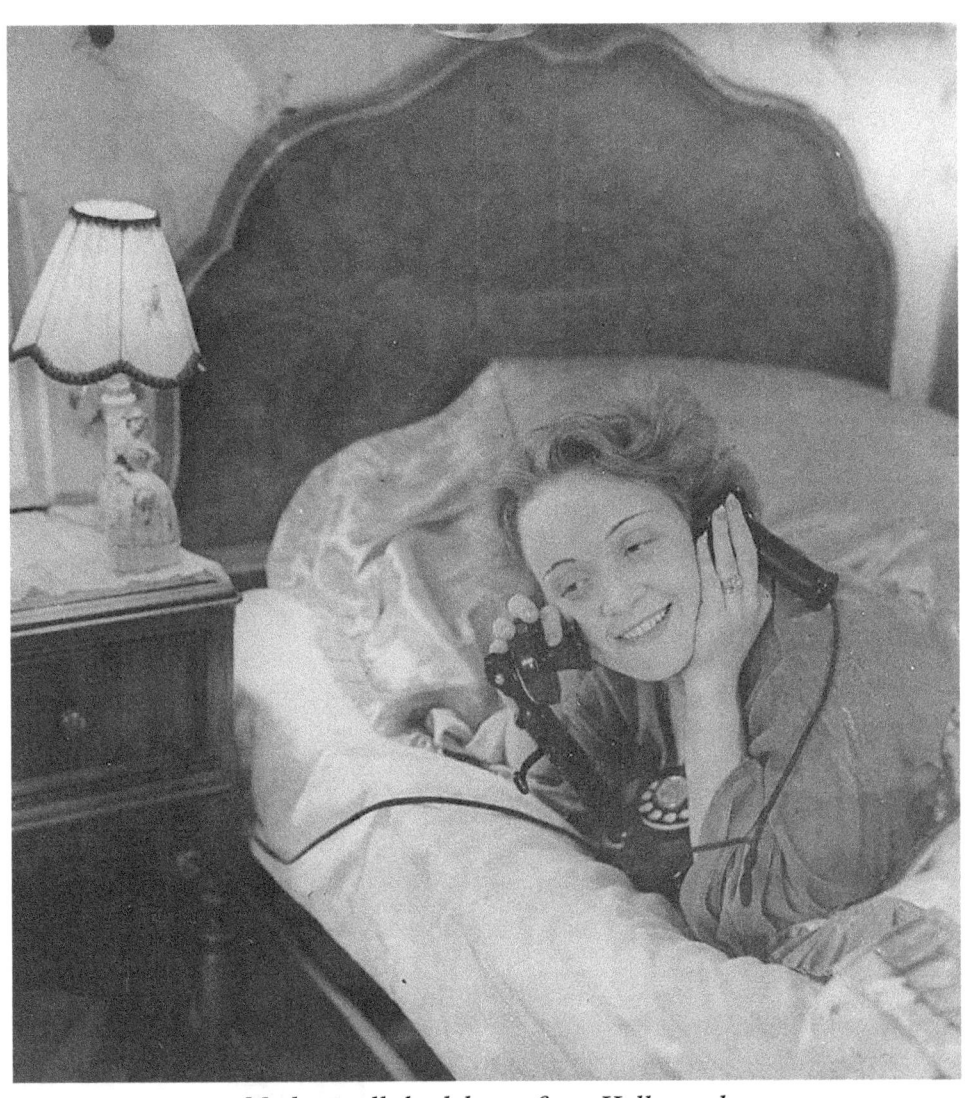

Marlene calls back home from Hollywood

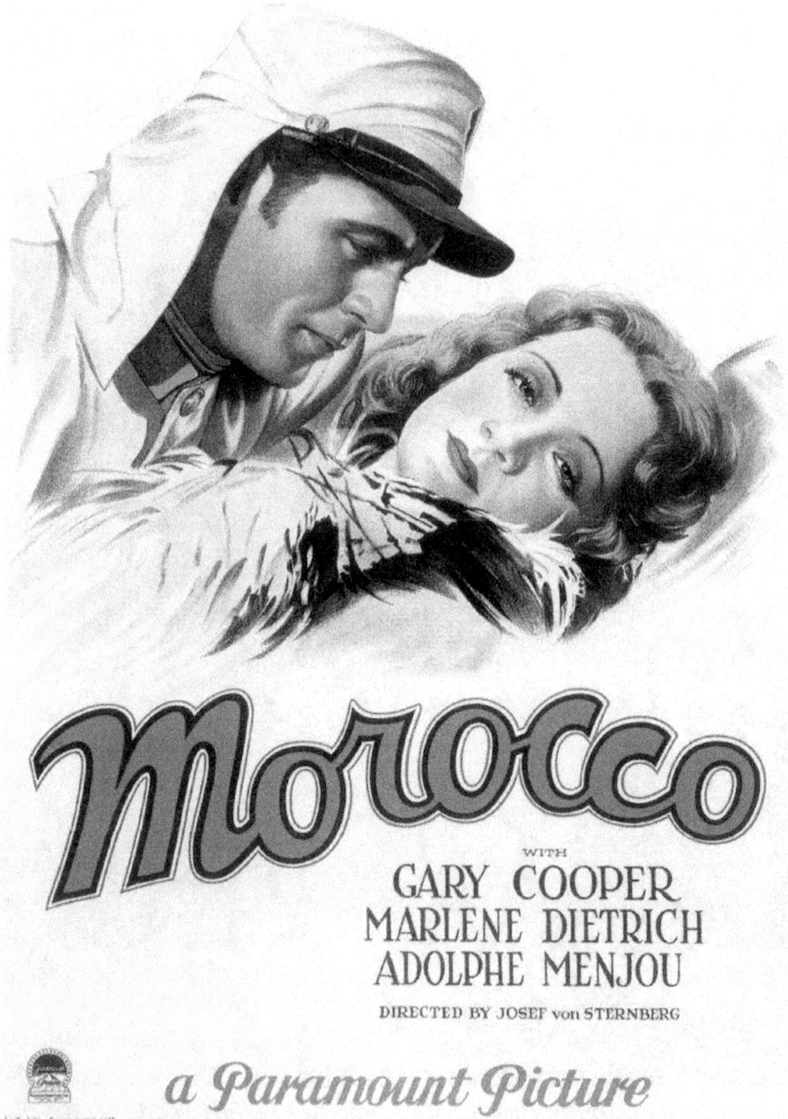

Morocco

WITH

GARY COOPER
MARLENE DIETRICH
ADOLPHE MENJOU

DIRECTED BY JOSEF von STERNBERG

a Paramount Picture

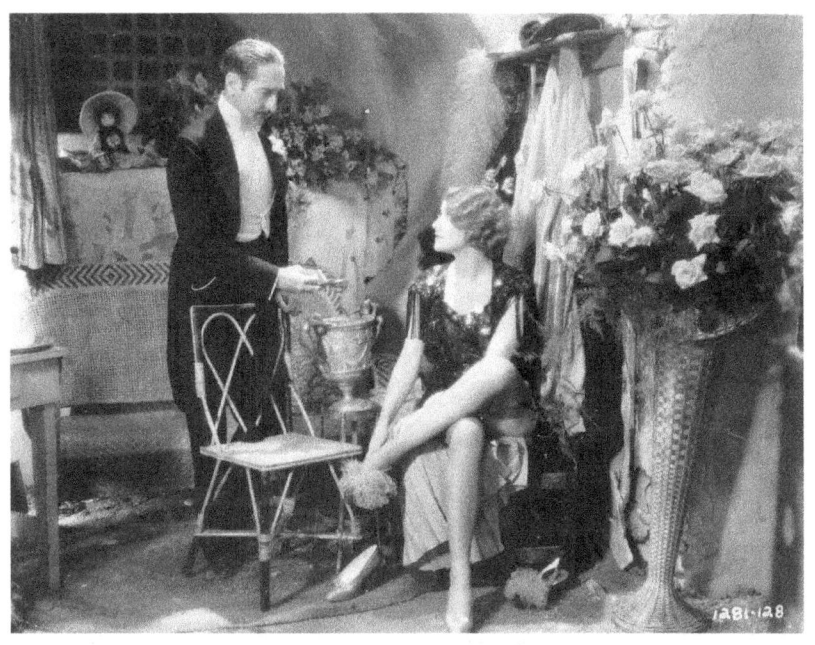

MOROCCO (1930)

If The Blue Angel planted the roots of the legendary Dietrich, then Morocco was when the myth began to grow and bloom into something quite wonderful. Morocco itself was already in fruition before The Blue Angel was even released, and Paramount Pictures were well aware, prophetically at least, that Marlene was hot property and destined for stardom. Sternberg left Germany before the premiere of The Blue Angel for the bright lights of Hollywood, and Dietrich herself soon followed, after studio boss B.P. Schulberg was impressed by Marlene's Lola-Lola test footage. The image of Dietrich heading for movie land, leaving her daughter behind, with a cargo of luggage, has entered movie history myth, and remains a vital part of the Marlene story and her rise to success. She was thrust into the spotlight, raved up in the press as the hottest new star of the day, a new Garbo in fact, an import destined for stardom. Remarkably, Dietrich was hyped up as a star before The Blue Angel was even released, and she was accepted by the public with no questions asked. By the time Morocco appeared, fans were already flocking to see her in the theatres; by the time they left, they knew they would never forget the name of Marlene Dietrich.

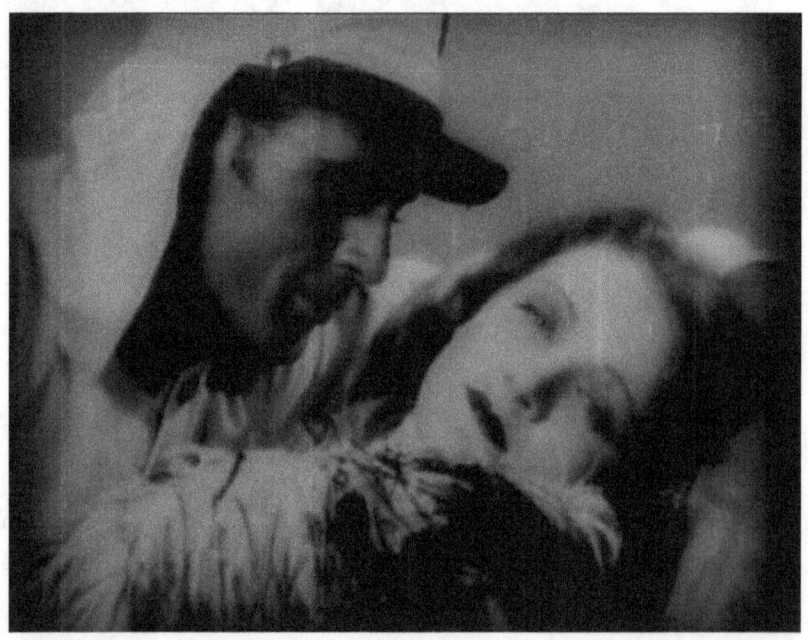

In Morocco, Dietrich plays nightclub singer Amy Jolly, one of the passengers on a ship heading to Morocco, along with La Bessiere (Adolphe Menjou) who shows interest in Jolly. We are introduced to Tom Brown (Gary Cooper), a private in the army who enjoys Jolly's provocative stage act. Appearing in top hat and tails, Dietrich performs When Love Dies, kisses a woman on the lips and hands over her key to Tom, who later visits her house where they strike up a fondness for one another. Unbeknownst to him, he is being observed by the husband of his former lover, who just happens to be Tom's commanding officer, Caesar. He and Jolly are set about in the street by two thugs hired by Caesar, but Tom wins the fight. What follows is an old fashioned, at times hopelessly corny love story, with Tom almost losing Jolly to the rich La Besseriere.

Like all of Dietrich's finest films, the lasting impression of Morocco is in the moments, the iconic stand outs rather than the whole film itself. Though it has a plot that we are seriously invested in - even if we are aware it's all rather silly in a charming way - it is Dietrich who remains the reason we stick around. It isn't just Dietrich herself that we are glued to however, it is the very idea of Dietrich and the way she is presented to us. It's as if von Sternberg is unveiling some great work of art, a creation he is proud of and wants to show the world. She was arresting enough in The Blue Angel, but already in Morocco - a short span of time since her debut - the familiar, iconic Marlene of film legend has arrived. She has that look about her, slender, with almost pointed cheek bones and sharp features, the face that could stop traffic and eyes that say more with a glance than a whole page of dialogue. It's not so much about acting but owning the screen. From her opening number, Dietrich is charisma personified, not as giddy and naively playful as she was as Lola-Lola, but more sophisticated, therefore more irresistible. Her performance in top hat and tails may be overly familiar to many film buffs, but the decades since its release have not dimmed the magic of that sequence. It is sexy, subversive and beautifully performed, certainly one of the most

31

important moments of pop culture from the whole of the 20th Century.

Though Dietrich's films often drip with innuendo, one notices the power of suggestion in Morocco beneath the surface, a much more subtle film than The Blue Angel. Cooper and Dietrich's romance is at the centre of the film, but they do not even speak to one another until some way into the film, making the whole thing a tease. But this works in the movie's favour, for just as Cooper feels the tension in Dietrich's seductive act and persona, so do us the viewers, putting us right beside the romantic lead in viewing Marlene as a seemingly unobtainable goddess.

Of course, all the credit cannot go to Dietrich, as appealing and magnetic as she may be. Undoubtedly the film would be much less without the visual imagination of Josef von Sternberg, and the lighting he perfected for Dietrich's angular features with the aid of Lee Garmes, the cinematographer. Sternberg once made a statement which summed up his whole career: "I care nothing about the story, only how it is photographed and presented. Shadow is mystery and light is clarity. Shadow conceals - light reveals. To know what to reveal and what to conceal and in what degrees to do this is all there is to art." Indeed, this could be his mantra, for in his movies with Dietrich the stories are often so oddly structured, ever winding and often erratic that they become secondary to the visuals. In fact, quite often, the more ludicrous they become (think the developments in the later Dishonoured for example) the more enjoyable the films become simply because the images are more striking. Quite often in a Dietrich/Sternberg movie you will come across a visual so arresting it could be framed and hung on a wall. Sternberg clearly thought in these terms, not as a storyteller but a visual stylist. If he was a slave to the image alone, than part of that image was Dietrich, a woman so liberated by her free sexuality, yet paradoxically also handcuffed to Sternberg's obsessive dreams.

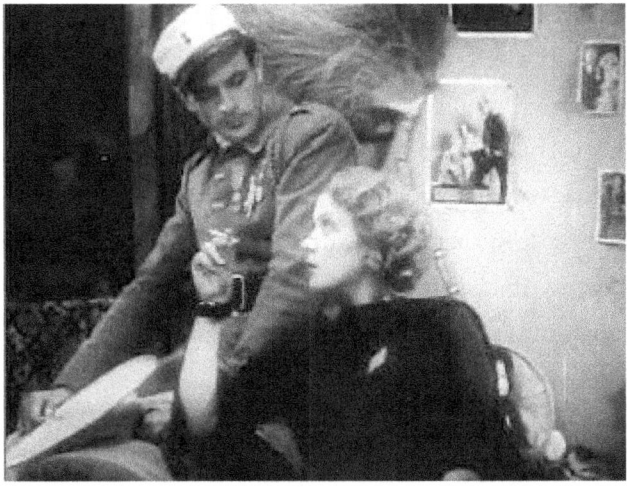

From here on, Sternberg and Garmes to a lesser extent knew how to capture the best of Dietrich. It was all about the angle of the light, illuminating her correctly so the viewer would immediately know the emphasis was on her over the rest of the cast. She is elevated, existing somewhere above the often inconsequential plot and in a realm of her own. It's in the shadows, the power of Dietrich through the lens of von Sternberg, as she slinks her way through the exotic, high camp surroundings. Even until the very end, with Dietrich on the Moroccan sand in a quest for her true love, von Sternberg is clear who our attention should be on, and just who out of the many actors in the film should live longest in our memories after the movie is over.

Today, Morocco, like many of Dietrich and von Sternberg's other films, is more known for the iconography than the story or film harbouring the legendary Dietrich stand outs. Images of her in the top hat have become so iconic that most people take the innovative qualities of Dietrich's part in the film for granted. But movie history is made up of single scenes and even single frames, moments which refuse to leave the public's consciousness despite the march of time. Dietrich's very appearance in Morocco, and even the publicity stills which show off her suggestive smirk with cigarette in hand, are enough to ensure that if not the film then at least Dietrich's Amy Jolly is firmly imbedded into film legend. In a way it almost doesn't matter that most people will pass on seeking out a film like Morocco and be more satisfied with the image and idea of Dietrich, the romanticised movie-still preserved in sepia, than the walking, talking, moving Dietrich on celluloid. At least in this way her legend lives on healthily, if only superficially.

Film scholars and academics have often written of the biblical subtext in Morocco, a thin concept it must be said, mostly borne out of the scene when Dietrich is handing out apples after her performance and the jokes in song which apparently allude to an Adam and Eve symbolism beneath the surface. But I don't feel one needs to perform such an academic study of a film like Morocco, which is purely a stylistic slice of escapism, especially if one comes out with a theory which would have made Dietrich roll her eyes impatiently. What matters is the film, but more so the images, those preserved visuals, with von Sternberg as painter of masterpieces and Dietrich as his muse.

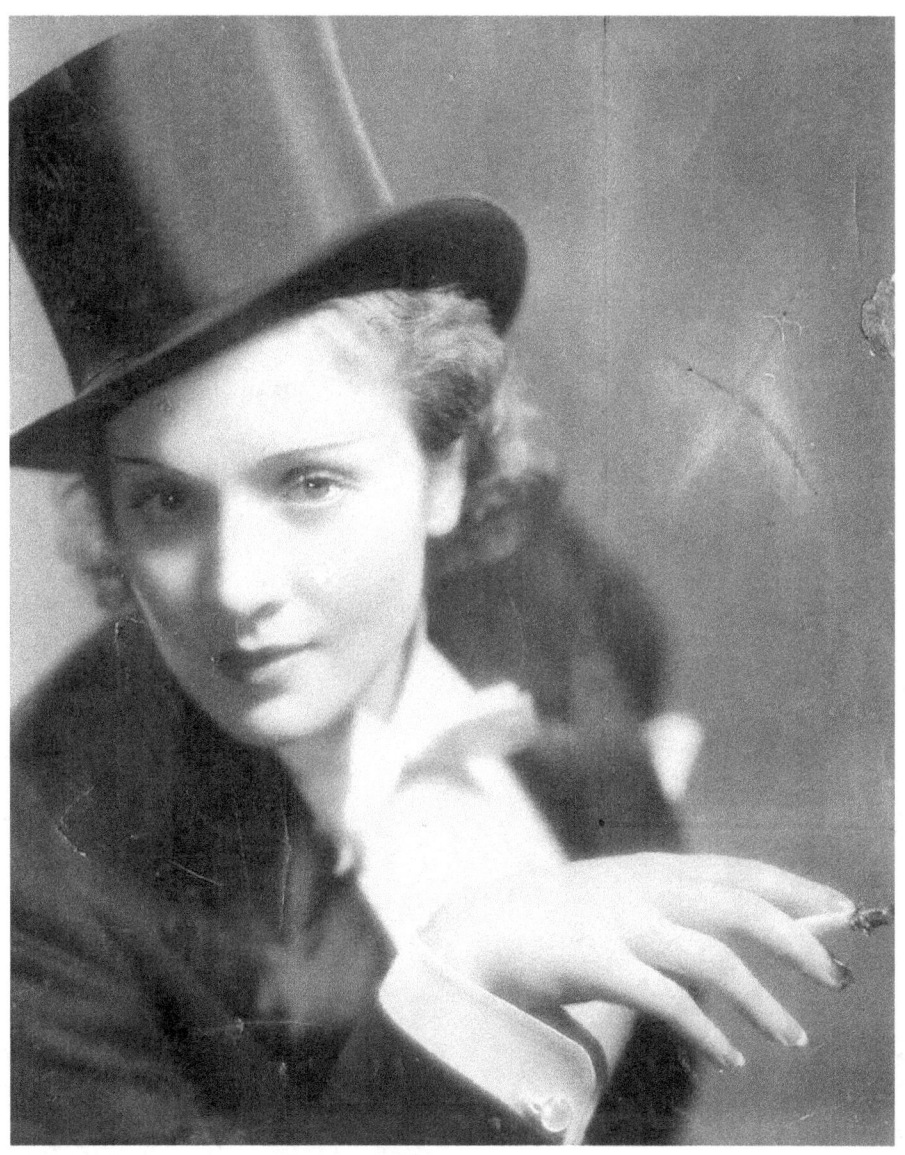

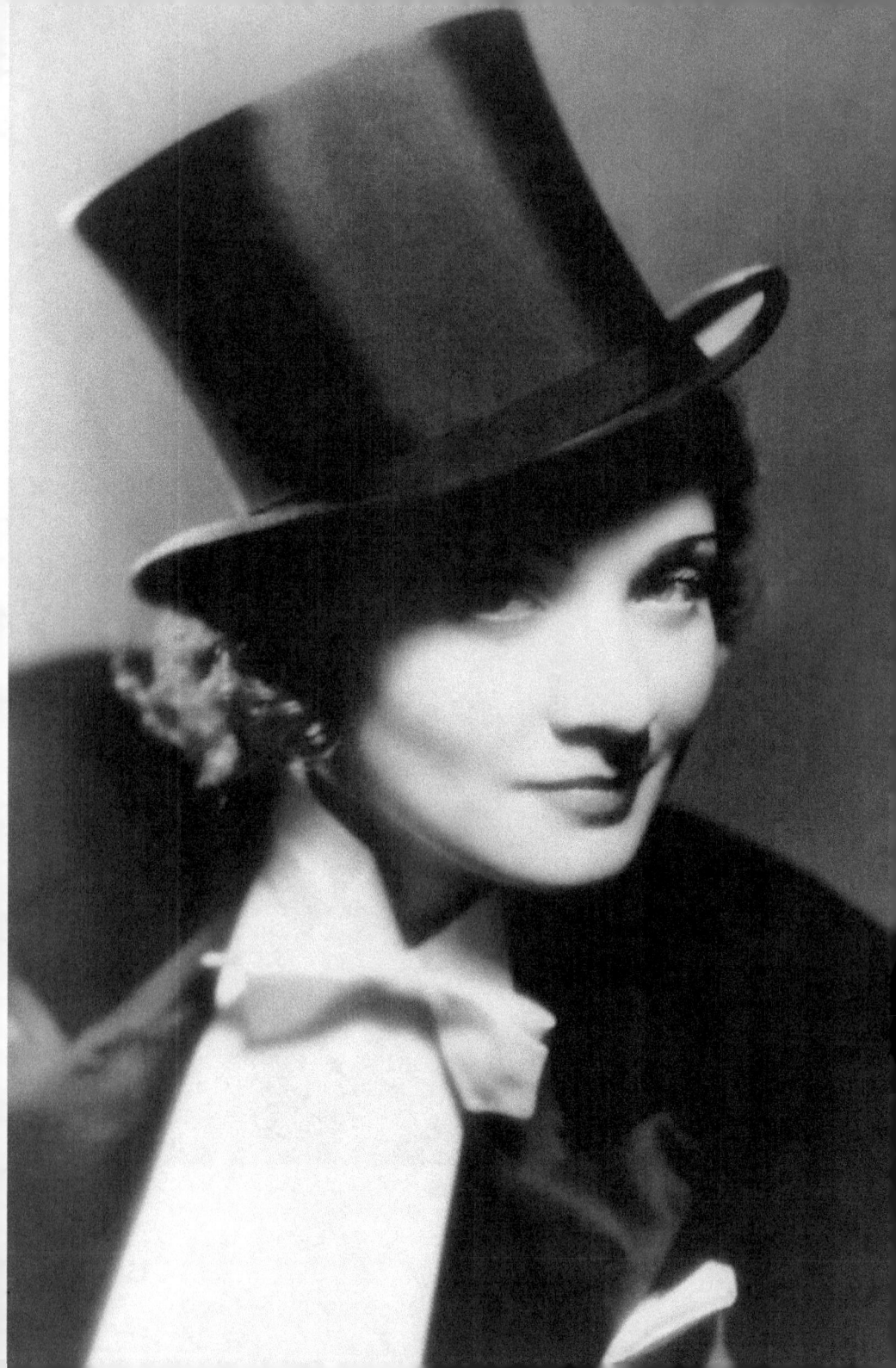

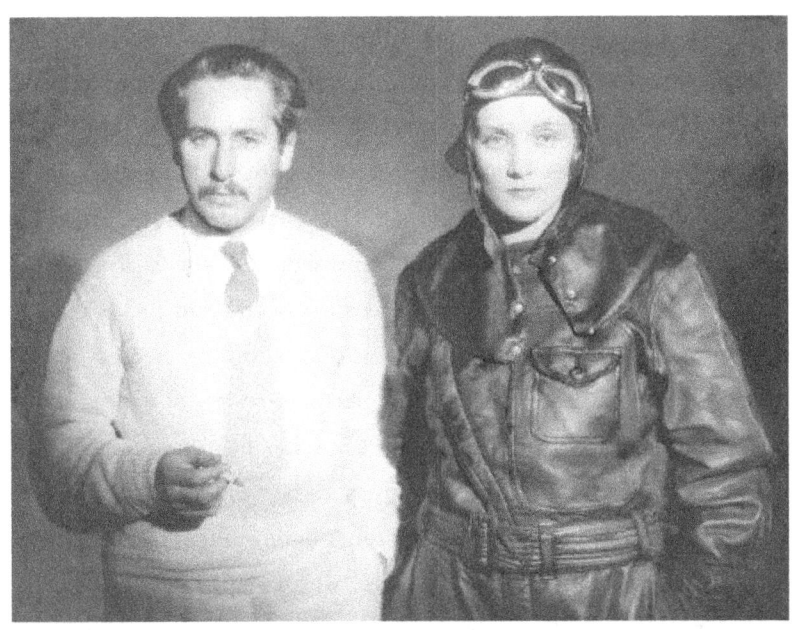

DISHONOURED (1931)

Dishonoured, though in some ways perhaps the most interesting collaboration between Dietrich and von Sternberg, is probably the least celebrated and talked about of their seven films, with he as visionary and she as idolised icon. Coming after The Blue Angel and Morocco, both of which established Dietrich as the ultimate object of desire, Dishonoured takes her glamorous persona a stage further and turns her into a myth. It is here that Dietrich the great untouchable being comes into her own.

The film itself begins beautifully, illustrating von Sternberg's knack of capturing stark visuals, here of the harsh, rainy, unforgiving city, with heavy dissolves and imaginative camera movements. We zone in on Vienna, during the war in 1915, one rainy night in particular as a body is being taken out of a block of flats in the red light district of the city. As the crowd gathers, it is clear the corpse is a prostitute who has taken her own life. Enter Dietrich, a fellow night prowler who declares "I am not afraid of life, although I am not afraid of death either." Our first sight of Dietrich is, of course, her legs (*those* legs I should add), and immediately she is a figure of great mystery and appeal. As she flees the scene and heads back to her lodgings, she is followed by the Chief of the Secret Service (Gustav von Seyfferitz), intrigued by her poetic view of existence. He sees potential in Dietrich, and seeing as he has been searching for an attractive woman to sign up as a spy, sees her as an ideal candidate. With the chief masquerading as a foreign agent to test her loyalty for her country, she alerts the police who then take him away, convincing the chief that as she stayed loyal, as he suspected, she will make a great spy.

Dietrich is known as Frau, a war widow with an apartment full of interesting knick knacks, a beloved black cat and a piano, which she plays brutally in the first apartment scene. The piano will return to the plot later as Frau illustrates her skill on the instrument. When she is summoned to the main headquarters of the Secret Service, the chief gives her the spy code name of X 27, and sets her to work. Her opening mission is to reveal two spies at a masked ball, a great sequence bordering on the purely surreal, in which Dietrich succeeds with flying colours. She ends up on the Polish border to sneak out Russian military plans, but her methods are criticised by Captain Kranau (Victor McLagen) who disapproves of her using sexuality and her feminine graces to achieve her goals.

In a sequence which illustrates Dietrich's under- valued acting range, she poses as a peasant girl in Russia working as a chambermaid, with her loyal feline by her side of course. The plot thickens, as a musical score acts as a secret code. Eventually, in an unexpected turn, X 27 is convicted of treason and sentenced to death. Though we presume the young soldier who has a soft spot for her may reverse the decision, he does not have such power, and the execution is acted out brutally and without empathy, sending Dietrich, riddled with bullets (though with no signs of blood thankfully), flying to the ground like a broken marionette.

When it came to plot, most of von Sternberg and Dietrich's films were ridiculous, though it was the kind of ridiculous we tend to enjoy. In fact, the more ludicrous the story line got, the more potential there was for von Sternberg to place his elegant muse in all manner of scenarios and settings. Dishonoured, with its far out story that though meandering at times delivers a fatal final punch that blows away all the preceding convolution, offers Dietrich so much as an actress but more importantly as a star. It's a showcase for her as a movie idol yes, but it also shows off her more varied abilities as a visual centre piece, the kind of which cinema history has chosen to sideline in favour of the spoilt rich glamour goddess image. She is not degraded as an object but elevated as a wonder. This is an important distinction.

It is clear from their third film together that von Sternberg is not so much in love with his star, but obsessed with her. Unable to own and possess her in real life, he perversely tortures himself in the films by elevating her ever higher, ensuring she is unobtainable. There is a masochistic tendency here, though von Sternberg would never have admitted the fact he worshipped Dietrich. Instead he put in older characters who acted as von Sternberg doppelganger cuckolds, men who knew that Dietrich was out of their grasp. His obsession with Marlene though, often overshadows anything that happens in the film around or behind her, and from beginning to end it is she who remains our focal point.

The vision and style may be von Sternberg's, but the film really belongs to Dietrich herself. She admitted that von Sternberg was the man who made her and without him she would never have become the Dietrich we all know and love, but there is undoubtedly a natural glow around her that movie lights and sets, not to mention costumes and hair styles, only enhance. In every scene she is set up to stun the viewer, to grab the attention, and indeed, even when doing a little tired stretch in her apartment, hinting to the Chief that it's time for him to go, she oozes sex appeal. But there is also humour present, suggesting that Dietrich is not taking herself entirely seriously. There is an added comedic value to the piano scenes, especially when a frantic Dietrich is hammering away at the tune, then turning swiftly to the sheer amazement at the group of men gathered round her, helpless as animals, as she de-codes the message. The word camp is thrown around a lot these days, and in the way Christopher Isherwood meant it, Dietrich and von Sternberg's Dishonoured is high camp. The masked ball scene, the maid sequence and in particular the striking execution, are all heavily stylised yet retain their individual power. Ludicrous yes, but never laughable.

There is also the fact that, like The Blue Angel, Dietrich is a vision of female empowerment, just as she was, admittedly in more varied ways, in future collaborations with von Sternberg. In Shanghai

Express she reduces all men to dribbling wrecks with her sexuality; in Blonde Venus she was frowned upon for abandoning the supposed rigidity of motherhood and family life, but came out a revolutionary female all the same; here she proves that as a spy she can more than match the men, even if her grisly fate suggests she will never be truly equal in the eyes of the system. Again though, Dietrich doesn't need a man, even if society tells her she does. As X 27 she is strong, powerful in fact, self assured and confident in a male dominated world. Though she is unfairly put to death, she does not shed a tear or show a hint of fear as the guns raise towards her. Until her dying moment she retains her dignity, yet the subsequent coldness felt by the males who took her life, leaving the room while the bullets still echo, is so unsettling that it makes one wonder if her struggle was worth it.

Plot and film so often became secondary to the star in Hollywood's Golden era, but here it seems more than ever the film exists mostly for its glamorous star. That said, Dietrich's glow robs nothing from the director, and von Sternberg uses every opportunity to show off his skills, to linger on visuals few other directors of the time, especially American filmmakers, would even dream of. Yes, focus is mostly on Dietrich's magical prowess, but she is aided by fascinating surroundings, captured beautifully by a von Sternberg in full control.

In 1968 von Sternberg wrote that he directed actors "by producing perhaps a trance, a sort of mesmerism otherwise unknown, by blotting out their traits and substituting a behaviour alien to them, by gesture and mimicry, by the drama of light and shade, by foiling every obstruction, by movement and angle of the camera, by constant alertness to voice and cadence, and most important of all—by inspecting oneself."

This trance is evident in other Dietrich collaborations, mostly Shanghai Express, but it's present in Dishonoured too. There is no need for background music, or extravagant indulgences that Hollywood's hired men would have employed. Josef lends the film an unreal quality, with actors as machines almost, creating a film which is hypnotic, soothing even, otherworldly at times. Dietrich, with her strange, individual voice and quirky way of delivering the English dialogue, lends herself to the dream-like world wonderfully, giving the feeling one is in a state of beautiful, heavenly delirium.

The film was rushed into production by Paramount after the high smash success of The Blue Angel and Morocco, based on the story of the infamous Dutch spy Mata Hari. Josef himself objected to the title which was chosen, insisting that X 27 was never dishonoured as the posters suggested. Though he felt this betrayed his vision of Dietrich, the female among the alpha males who died with honour rather than dishonour, von Sternberg did not have the power to override Paramount's decisions. Ever one to compete, MGM panicked at the sight of Dietrich as the Hari-esque spy and speedily put together a project starring her "rival", Greta Garbo, more successful at the box office but today much more dated.

Considering the many joys of Dishonoured, especially for fans of simply basking in Dietrich's beauty, Dishonoured is still one of the least appreciated of her collaborations with von Sternberg. When it is mentioned in David A Cook's A History of Narrative Film, it gets a quick summarisation as "sardonic and not particularly inspired", which seems misinformed.

If the film hasn't endured as one of her widely loved movies, it was nicely received in some quarters in the day, at least by those who understood Dietrich's appeal. In Richard Watts' review he wrote "of Miss Dietrich, it need only be said that she proves once more that her hasty ride to film celebrity was the result of neither luck or publicity. There still may be some doubt whether she possesses that technical expertness on which so many observers place such store, but there can be little question by now that her almost lyrically ironic air of detachment and, to be frank, her physical appeal, make her one of the great personages of the local drama."

In his book on Dietrich, Homer Dickens wrote that the role was "perfectly suited to the Dietrich face, manner, voice and style. This offered more acting range than Dietrich had thus far known under von Sternberg. She was not only creating varying moods, but was letting herself be created within those moods. Thus we see many Dietrichs in the film."

While it may have its admirers, Dishonoured is one of those Dietrich gems drifting more and more into obscurity, into the dusty vaults so to speak. But has its fans it certainly does. This intoxicating spell of a film remains as bewitching now as no doubt it was back in 1931.

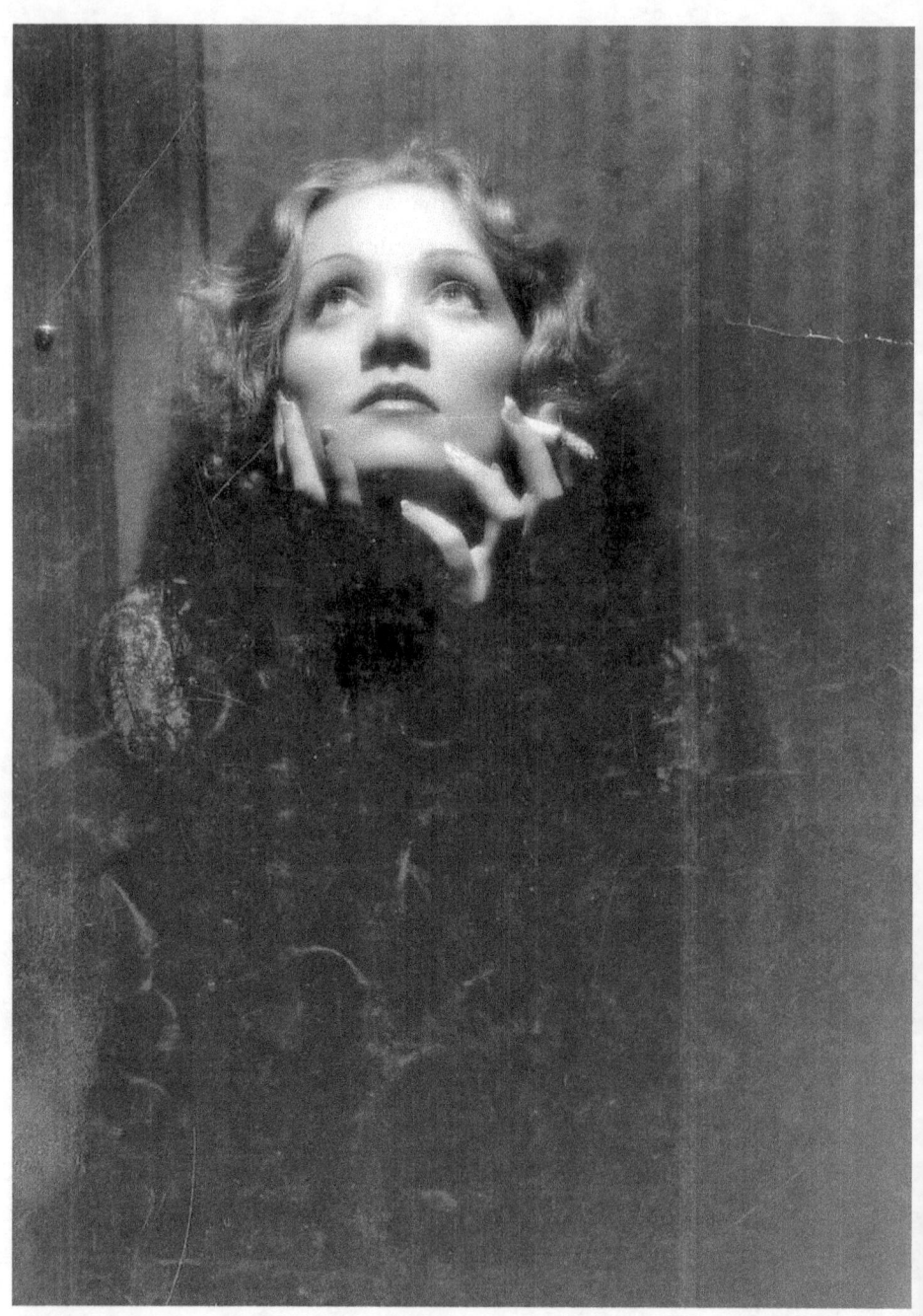

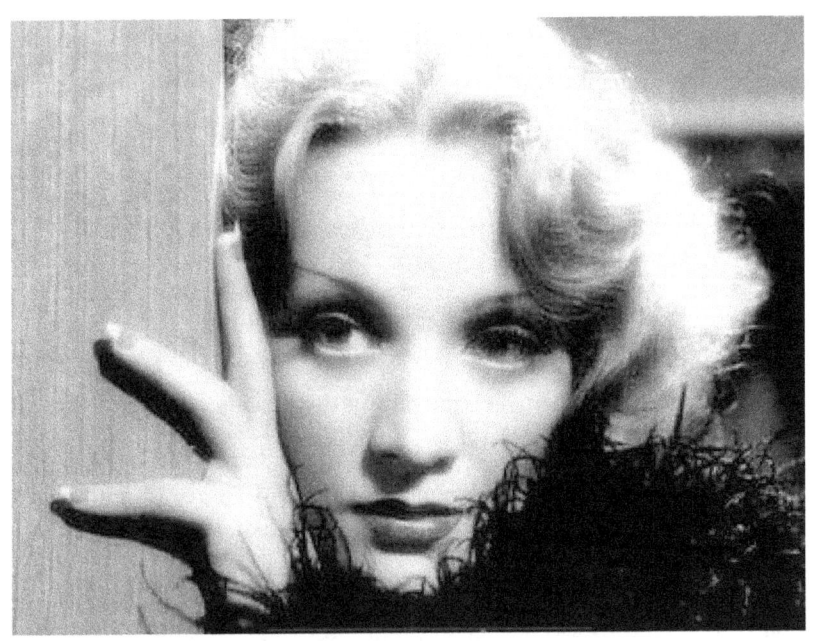

SHANGHAI EXPRESS (1932)

Shanghai Express is widely considered to be the pinnacle of Dietrich and von Sternberg's collaborations. Some of the other films they made together may be superior in other areas, yet in regards to presenting as Dietrich as perfect idol, a glamour icon completely out of reach to us mere mortals, Shanghai Express has no competition. It was also the biggest commercial success of the Dietrich and von Sternberg pictures, making nearly 4 million at the time in the US alone; clearly, an America suffering during the Great Depression found Dietrich and her immortal beauty a most satisfying distraction.

Shanghai Express is based on the story by Henry Harvey, concerning a train heading from Peking to Shanghai during the Chinese Civil War in 1931. Clive Brook plays British Captain Donald

Harvey, whose friends tell him he will be sharing the train with the famous Shanghai Lily, played by Dietrich, who actually turns out to be a former lover named Madeline, with whom he enjoyed a passionate affair before she was known around the world under her new pseudonym. Their affair had ended five years earlier when a ploy set up by Lily resulted in him leaving her, but as is clear from their first meeting together, there are still feelings between the pair.

We are also introduced to other passengers on the express train, such as Lily's friend Hui Fei, played by the terrific Anna May Wong, eccentric English woman Mrs Haggerty (Louise Closser Hale in a dotty performance) and the strange, mistrustful Henry Chang, who is portrayed by Warner Oland.

A plot soon develops when the Chinese Government come on board in search of a rebel leader, and later on, thanks to Chang who sends a message out, the train is taken over by the rebel army, the leader of whom is Chang himself, who suddenly turns out to be a much more sinister character than we first thought. Chang discovers that Captain Harvey is on his way to perform surgery on the Governor General of Shanghai, so needs him alive. Meanwhile Chang has his eyes on making Shanghai Lily his mistress, who uses his infatuation with her in a secret scheme to free the express train from the vicious rebels.

Oddly, when written out, the plot seems more exciting and engaging than it actually is on screen. The way von Sternberg paces the film and its thin storyline is rather unusual, in that the dialogue itself and the way it is delivered is flat, almost robotic in fact. The truth is that von Sternberg encouraged this mechanical way of speaking to emulate the rhythms of the train. It may make for a slightly odd, disjointed viewing, but the voices and mannerisms do indeed blend in with the chugging grind of the engine. Acted in this way, the plot never feels sensational or unbelievable. Yes the film has a strangely surreal air to it, thanks to the performances, but there is no dramatic music, no flamboyant camera movements to enhance any of the action, and there is never a sense of phony heightened excitement. Indeed, Shanghai Express is as steady and immovable as the grind of the train the characters are on board.

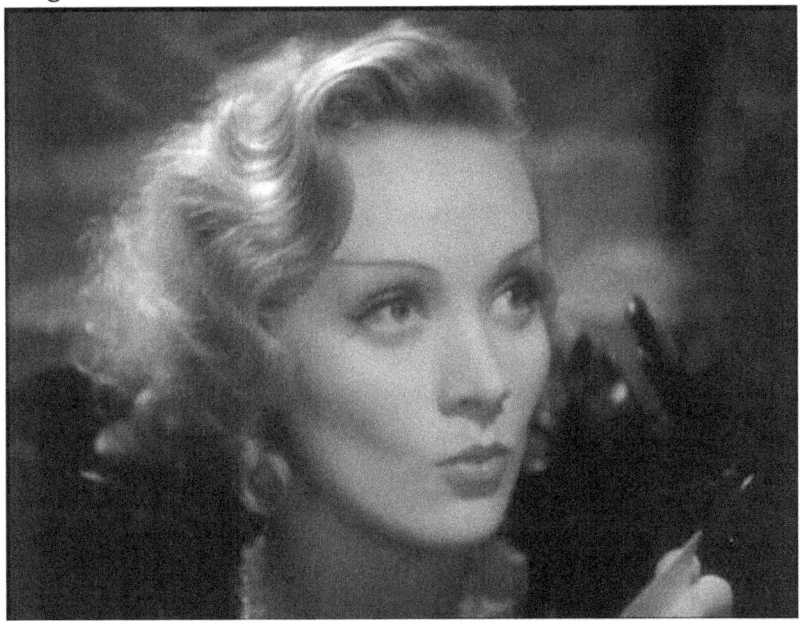

Paramount Pictures knew that a von Sternberg and Dietrich picture would always be costly, because costumes, lighting and sets had to look a certain way and von Sternberg himself insisted on taking his time to achieve what he had set out to. They weren't always guaranteed hits of course (some of their other movies had been disappointments at the box office) but Paramount seemed happy enough to let the director indulge himself, as well as his most vivid fantasies. And let's face it, von Sternberg's most vivid fantasy, his wildest infatuation, his true obsession, was Marlene Dietrich herself.

This brings us to what is at the epicentre of this whole exercise in style and mood, Marlene, his goddess of glamour, whose very presence dominates the film. Everything that happens, every word, every line, every scene, every costume, every lavish set, and every set up is to lend gravitas to the arrival of Dietrich. When she's not on camera the viewer is thinking about when she will appear next, and when she's being filmed in all her glory we cannot take our eyes off her. If von Sternberg's aim was to make a fetishistic item out of not just Dietrich herself but the very idea of her, then he succeeded.

Not so much as acting but more just "being" in the purest sense, Marlene is the embodiment of old style movie star charisma. Her exotic looks dazzle, her costumes hang on to her slender frame and her lines, often purred seductively, often spoken in that classic disjointed Dietrich manner, come forth like mini quotable nuggets, not realistic in any way, but highly memorable for that fact alone. When she isn't speaking, Dietrich is a walking - or still-standing - work of art for the ever hungry von Sternberg, who seemed to get a thrill out of placing her in increasingly bizarre circumstances and positions. Shanghai Express is a film yes, one with a plot that while easy to follow is still properly worked out, but for the most part this is movie not just as moving painting, but as showcase for Dietrich. She is gorgeous and radiant.

It's worth noting that critics and admirers say it was Shanghai Express that made her a glamour icon and firm household name, and it's fair to say that it wasn't the film itself that enhanced her popularity but her appearance, or even more specifically, her presentation, unveiled as she is like a great timeless masterpiece, within the picture itself. This was the fourth time von Sternberg and Dietrich had worked together, and by now he was an expert in Dietrich lighting. With Dietrich it was all about shadows, the spaces, where to place lights to accentuate her looks, her lips, her cheekbones, and perhaps most vitally of all, her legs. It might be wrong to call Dietrich's work in Shanghai Express a performance, for it is more of a reveal, an act of showmanship, a magic act in some regards, and a master class in effortlessly stealing scenes by just being present. Yes she was aided by a director who knew his star's best angles, and a brilliant cinematographer, Lee Games, who won an Academy Award for the film (Marlene later gave most of the credit to von Sternberg himself, who obviously guided the cinematography), but Dietrich's self control and knowledge of her own power were vital factors in this glamour tour de force. The impact is also aided by tension. Dietrich's first appearance in the film is through a veil which covers half her face. As if to tease and titillate the viewer, von Sternberg does not reveal the enigmatic Dietrich until she is on board. Before then she is spoken of with excitement, a mythical character in her own life time. Once we are on board the train, Lily becomes the focal point for our senses; the plot is secondary, and the other cast members standing by for the arrival of Dietrich's quietly towering presence. She does not need to try hard; she is effortlessly a star in every way.

Reviewers were impressed by the film upon its release, but most of all by Dietrich's star power. Many noted the control she had over her part and the audience. The New York Times praised her, writing,

"Miss Dietrich gives an impressive performance. She is languorous but fearless as Lily. She glides through her scenes with heavy eyelids and puffing on her cigarettes. She measures every word and yet she is not too slow in her foreign-accented speech. Brooks' performance is also noteworthy, but he speaks in a monotone and is a little too hasty sometimes in his replies in conversations with Miss Dietrich."

Shanghai Express succeeds because it does not try to convince the viewer it is not a motion picture. This is escapism pure and simple, beautifully lit and photographed in seductive black and white, tasteful and assured in every scene, with all emphasis on the appeal of Dietrich. Josef von Sternberg became well known for his slow dissolves, which though began to tire some people a few pictures in, are handled masterfully here. The way the sequences blend together makes the transitions natural, often seamless, compared to the often jarring quality of some early sound pictures. And though one can fairly say that the delivery of the dialogue may put off modern viewers (there is, after all, almost a complete lack of emotion in the film), anyone with the patience to enjoy this film for what it is will be convinced that the technique works brilliantly. If anything, the disjointed speaking enhances the fact that we are in von Sternberg's alternative world, a place where myth and reality blend together to create a kind of enhanced dream state, emotionally stunted yet stylistically controlled.

Modern viewers attuned to fast moving plots, breakneck paces and snappily delivered dialogue may find Shanghai Express painfully old fashioned and slow. For others however, the film will come across as a soothing escape from modernity, a film which though fairly short feels endless in the best possible way. To compliment the film further,

I would say that as soon as it finishes it would not be an odd choice to put it back on again, or to even having it showing in the background as you go about your day. There is a quality here that makes the movie a comforting pleasure, a treat. Shanghai Express is a classy, surrealistic distraction which may tread carefully through its flimsy plot, but does so with such grace that one wouldn't object to it being three hours long. The people and the words they speak blend wonderfully in with the visuals, as if being sucked into the hypnotism of the whole piece. We are in von Sternberg's fantasy now, and Dietrich is the queen of this hazy indulgence.

Though von Sternberg had made other great films together, and would do so again the same year with Blonde Venus, there is a quality to Shanghai Express which makes it so otherworldly, so unique in is flatness, which ensures it will remain their seminal collaboration. While other early talkies from the age seem jerky and irrelevant, Shanghai Express is timeless, a film for all the ages; and it is also vintage Dietrich, sure proof that she was perhaps the most appealing and watchable of all the classic female stars of the Golden era.

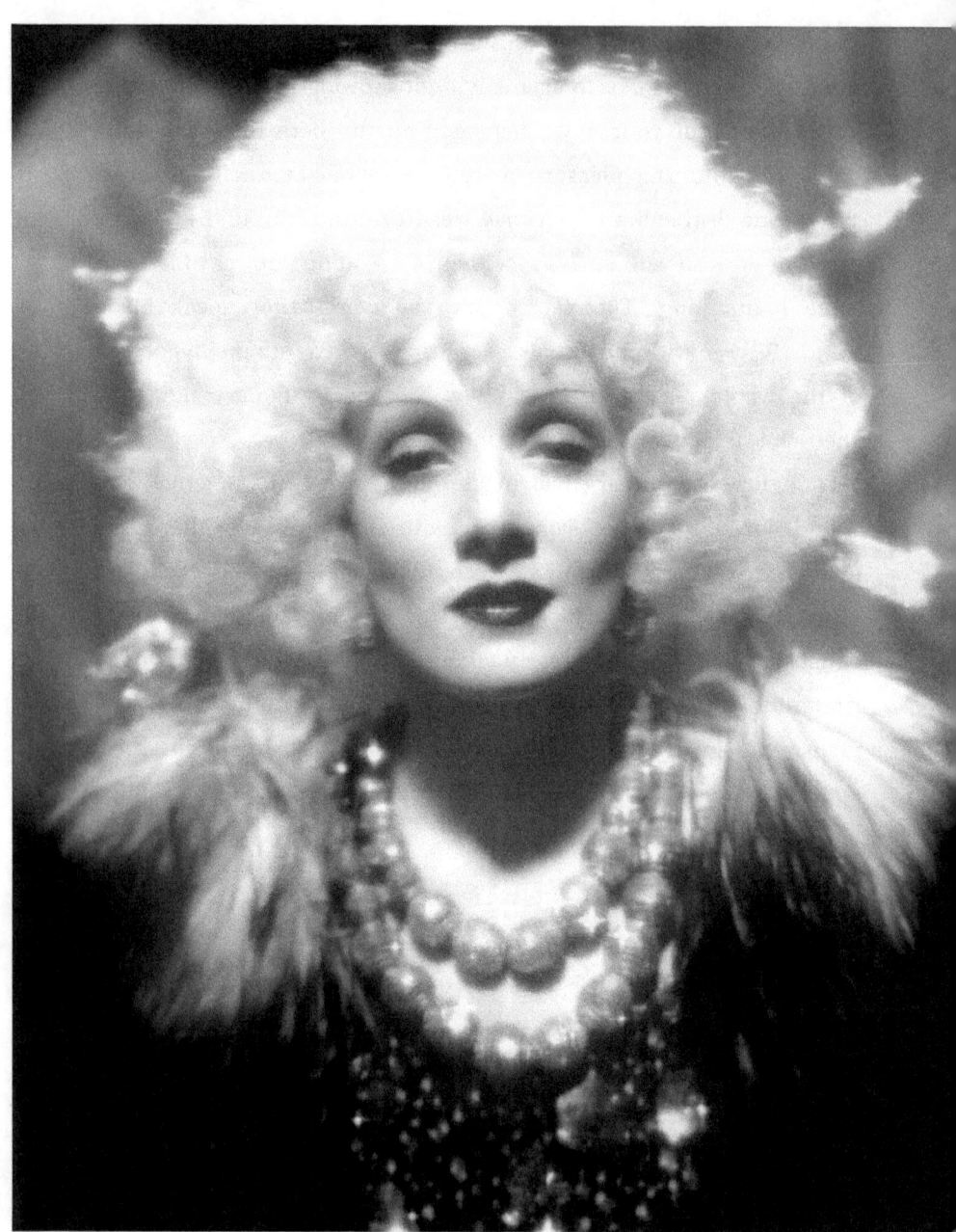

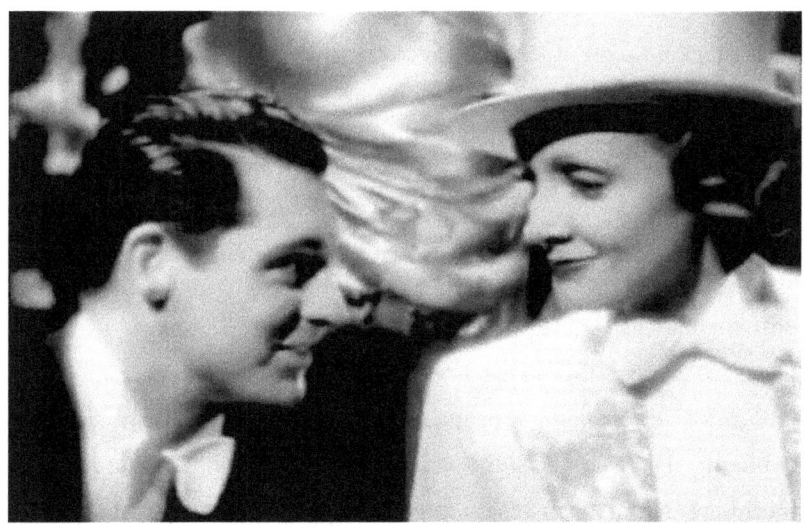

BLONDE VENUS (1932)

Blonde Venus marked a big change in Marlene Dietrich's on screen career. Granted, she was still centre stage as she had been in the previous four von Sternberg movies, but here her character moved further away from being von Sternberg's fetishist icon and towards a more proto-feministic direction. Blonde Venus, released the same year as Shanghai Express, still placed Dietrich as a figure of extreme glamour, but it also depicted her as a woman, a multi faceted character, and perhaps most importantly, a mother.

In the build up to her arrival in Hollywood and elevation to world stardom, Paramount's film publicity cunningly ensured that potential fans were reminded frequently that Dietrich was a family woman. She was depicted in interviews as being a devoted mother, and time and time again was photographed alongside her daughter Maria. Things were not as perfect as they seemed to be in reality, but the truth was that the public, one increasingly aware of Dietrich as a superstar and icon of beauty, loved the motherly side of Marlene. It's a surprise then that Paramount waited until her fifth Hollywood picture to properly depict her as a mother. In Blonde Venus she plays one role, but it's a well rounded one, not merely a caricature of idealised perfection and womanhood. She's a dancer yes, but she's also a loving wife, and a committed mother. This was a more three-dimensional Dietrich, slightly nudged if not removed from her pedestal. But was this a Dietrich the world was ready to accept?

Blonde Venus begins beautifully with a breathtaking sequence depicting Dietrich as some exotic water nymph, and again, von Sternberg has us at a distance gawping at her fabulousness. She is cavorting in a pond with five other girls, all naked, somewhere in Germany, watched over by seven American students. Helen (Marlene Dietrich), clearly the bluntest of the ladies, tells them all to clear off, though one man, Ned (played by Herbert Marshall) stubbornly refuses.

We then cut away, but water is a linking image. It is a few years later, and Dietrich, looking decidedly less glamorous, earthier perhaps, and in some ways more approachable (dare I say relatable?), is bathing a small boy in a bath. She and Ned ended up marrying and having a child, but their happy life together has been cut short by the news that Ned has been poisoned by radium and predicts he will be dead within a year. He visits a doctor who tells him that if he were willing to pay $1500 and travel across Germany he could meet a physician who may be able to cure him of this supposed death sentence.

Then there is a lovely scene of Ned and Helen putting their son to bed, with Marlene telling their son the story of how they met before singing a sweet song while winding up a music box as the boy drifts sweetly to sleep. Ned and Helen then discuss the matter of the expensive treatment, and Helen comes up with the idea of going back to the stage to raise the cash. Ned is hesitant if not outright objectionable to the idea, but in the end Helen goes along to a club to get theatre work as a performer. After performing her sensational and famous Hot Voodoo routine (where Dietrich comes on stage in an ape costume which she then removes) she meets Nick Townsend (Cary Grant), a rich politician who instantly has a thing for her. Though infatuated with Dietrich herself, he gives her $300 towards her husband's treatment.

Speedily, Dietrich has enough to pay the medical bills and though lying to her husband about where the money came from, she sends him off to the specialist. After she and her son see Ned off to sea, Nick arrives and gives her a lift home. He promises her free boarding at a friend's apartment, and won over by Nick's kindness, she begins to fall for him. Though she loves Ned, Helen agrees to go on vacation with Nick, just as Ned arrives home early from his treatment, where he finds his wife gone. Ned then discovers the truth of her quitting the stage and pairing up with Nick, promising to give her back every penny she earned for his treatment. When Ned says he will fight Helen for custody of their son, she fleas the house and goes on the run. She spends a large part of the film fleeing the police, and when she realises she is in too deep, that this restless fugitive existence is damaging for her son, she hands him over to Nick and goes on her way.

In a marvellous scene, Dietrich has a kind of breakdown where she throws all her money away by giving it to a down and out in a women's safe house. Though her prospects look bleak at this point, she picks herself up and hits the stage, where she ends up as a star in Paris. Reunited with Nick, she tells him how much she misses her son, and being a gentleman he is urged by his conscience to take her back home to America to be with her son. In a final scene, beautiful in its old fashioned purity and simplicity, a reunited Helen and Ned are putting their son to bed. Comforted by the sight of his parents together again, the boy asks to hear the tale of how they met. Helen winds up the same music box from the start of the film, which we see in a long close up which seems to reflect the merry go round journey we are all on in life, but especially Helen herself, who now realises home is where the heart is. Though she and Ned will not immediately return to how they once were, they both know that they belong with one another.

Blonde Venus takes Dietrich out of the stagey settings of her previous films and into the real world, all over a vast and dangerous America and then into a glamorous Paris. Her journey is an epic one of self discovery, an adventure into the world but also into herself. Despite all the travelling and performing, the promises of wealth from Nick and the life style he could have given her, she knows that simple little house, with Ned and her son by her side, is all that she needs. It may seem simplistic in the eyes of modern viewers, but the message is still valid and can be applied to life itself for all of us. The grass may look greener over yonder, but it's not so bad on this side either.

Strangely enough, it was this widening of the scope, turning Dietrich into a wild outlaw in the jungle of life, which prompted reviewers to cast their doubts on the Dietrich/Sternberg partnership.

The New York Times for instance wrote that Blonde Venus was a "muddled, unimaginative and generally hapless piece of work, relieved somewhat by the talent and charm of the German actress..."

The film was written by von Sternberg with S.K. Lauren and Jules Furthman, and it needs to be added that in his autobiography von Sternberg himself said it was written "swiftly to provide something other than the sob stories that were being submitted." Josef knew his star well enough to be sure that standard Hollywood claptrap, the aforementioned sob stories, would do Dietrich no good, and that she had to be in control of her circumstances, no matter what the role. Vitally it seems, Helen is at times lost and very much in need, but she never reaches out for a man's guidance. She may take money from Nick, but ultimately she is her own woman; so much so in fact that in the last part of the picture she is liberated from the burden of her son and takes to life as a sole entity, where, importantly it seems, she succeeds. She is no longer bogged down by the temptations from Nick, the neediness of Ned and her son. The Blonde Venus arrives when Helen is free enough to welcome her.

All this of course may have been hard for audiences in 1932 to accept. After all, in the eyes of backward thinking men, women belonged at home, and any female expressing a desire to do anything away from the stove was hushed. On screen, women were usually fancy frills, eye candy or love interest for the dashing heroic males. Dietrich then was way ahead of her time, especially in her von Sternberg films. One needs to only look at that run of films - Dishonoured which saw her as a spy put to death, Shanghai Express which had her as the ultimate male fantasy and Blonde Venus as a trailblazing feminist rebelling from the family constraints - to see she was a cut above the other female leads of the day. Unlike other actresses, she did not cry out for our sympathy, or even for us to like her. What Dietrich did though, through her charisma, was force us to at least care, and in Blonde Venus, a film that is nearly ninety years old, we root for her in her ragtag journey towards inner peace and acceptance.

As an actual film, in visual terms, Blonde Venus is not quite as stylish and slick as Shanghai Express, but it certainly had more in terms of content that its predecessor, if not in style. Express, as great as it is, was more of a showcase for Dietrich's poses, her enigmatic appeal, her exotic radiance etc. Blonde Venus however showed her not just as a beautiful woman, but also as a mother, often unglamorous, and a very flawed woman. She was egocentric and ruthless, but in the end, for all her shortcomings, a decent human being at heart. The previous von Sternberg films lacked this depth. What Blonde Venus often lacks in frilliness it makes up for with story, its sense of exhausted desperation when she's on the run, and the more complex performance from Dietrich. On top of that of course are the wonderful stage routines, with Dietrich excelling in the Hot Voodoo number and sizzling in her white top hat and tails sequence.

Cinematographer Bert Glennon does a great job with the film, making Dietrich look great even when in her ordinary, every day domestic setting. Dietrich may be seen as this unapproachable woman to whom household chores are a mystery, but she also pulls off her scenes as the doting mother and homemaker. At the same time, she still looks worthy of movie star idolisation, again this partly down to the photography.

On the other end of things, the song sequences are also photographed wonderfully well. At this stage, the world's image of Dietrich was already so firmly established that she looked like a true veteran in the stage sequences. This was down to her experience on the stage which went back over a decade, but it was also down to confidence; note her relaxed mood on the final song routine and you will see Dietrich is sure of herself and her immovable stardom. She must have known all too well that her name would now be forever known to the public.

Today, Blonde Venus is seen as one of the least notable of Marlene and Josef's collaborations, which seems unjustified when you consider what it has going for it; the songs are enough to ensure a legendary status, while the forward thinking slant on the free woman should if anything enhance its historical importance. Save for Hot Voodoo however, which often gets singled out as a career highlight (usually in reference to her innuendo laden songs) and the white tuxedo number (itself seen as a pale copy of the admittedly much sexier Morocco routine), Blonde Venus seems to have been largely ignored down the years. In the cult of Marlene however, it is a match for Shanghai Express and Morocco, illustrating the fact that Dietrich was much more than a pretty face well lit.

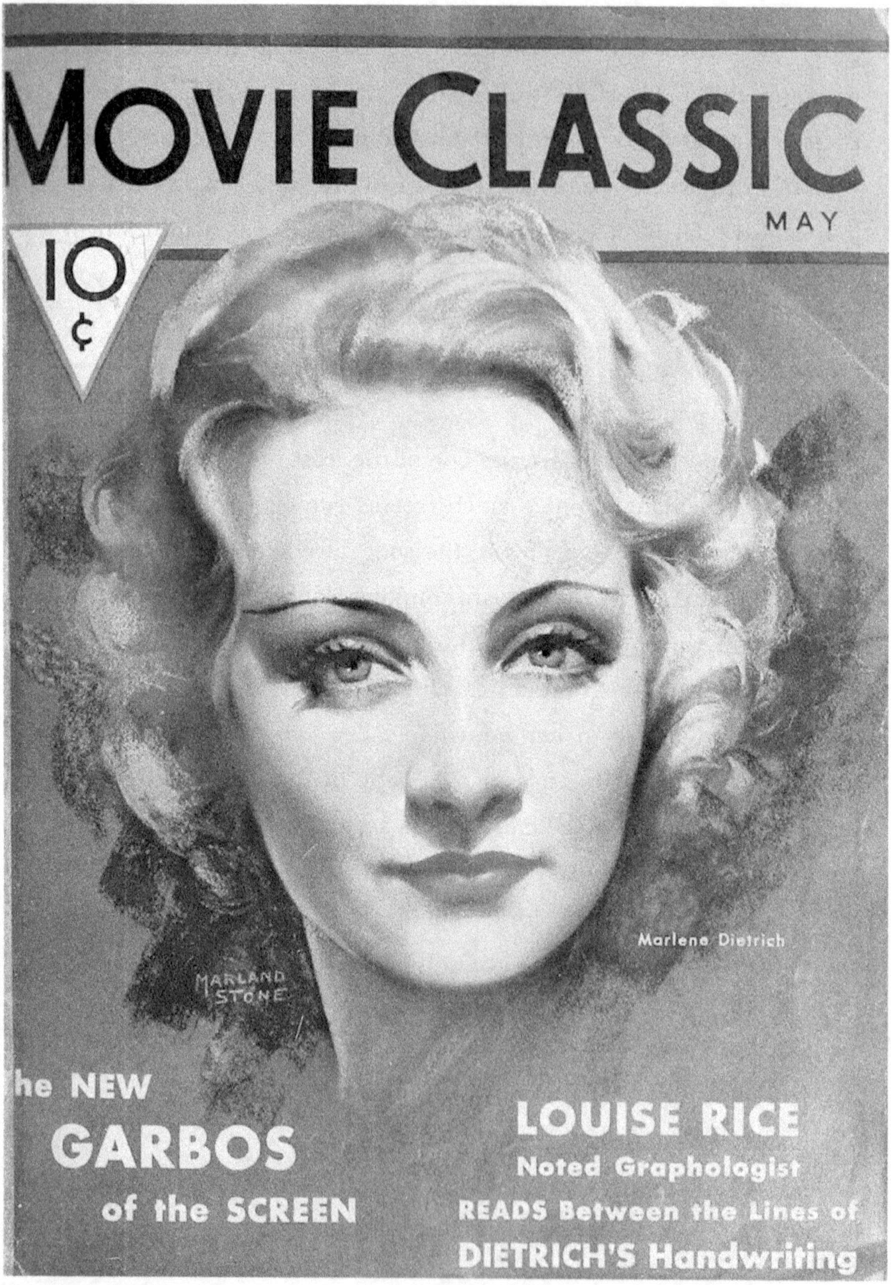

MOVIE CLASSIC

MAY

10¢

Marlene Dietrich

MARLAND STONE

The NEW
GARBOS
of the SCREEN

LOUISE RICE
Noted Graphologist
READS Between the Lines of
DIETRICH'S Handwriting

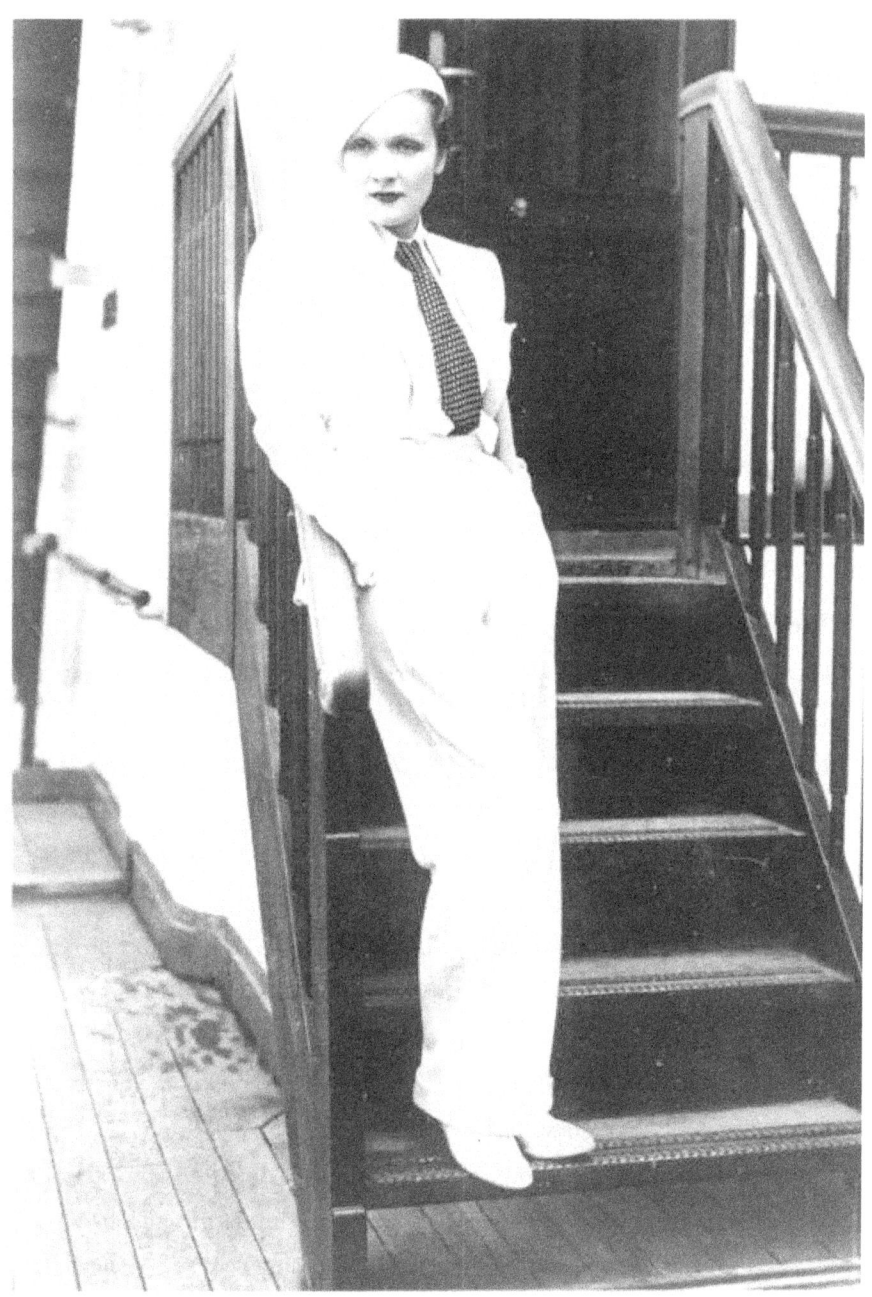

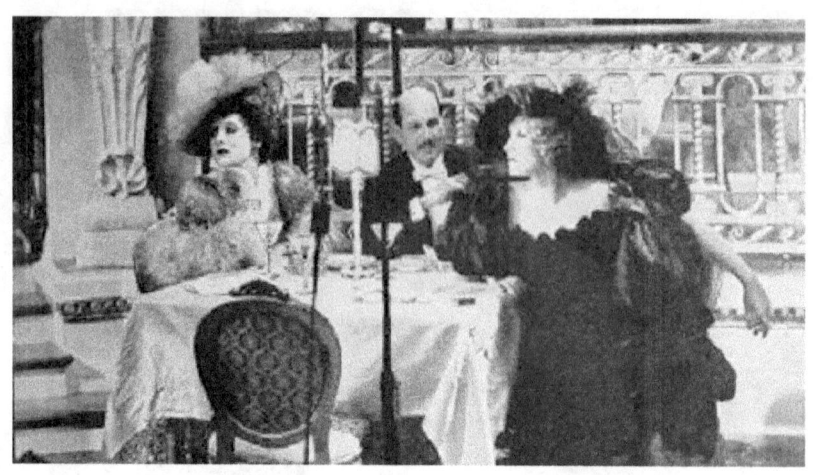

THE SONG OF SONGS (1933)

Marlene Dietrich's first American picture not directed by Josef von Sternberg was Song of Songs. This time she was under the guidance of Rouben Mamoulian, working from a script by Leo Brinskey and Samuel Hoffenstein, adapted from the play and novel of the same name. Here, Dietrich plays Lily (not Shanghai Lily of course), who arrives in Berlin to pose for Richard (Brian Aherne), a sculptor who lives across the street. The pair strike up a romance, but Lily ends up marrying a rich client of Richard's, the fittingly named Baron von Merzbach. However, the pull between Lily and Richard is too great, and love prevails.

Out of the safe but strangely constricting grip of von Sternberg, Dietrich adapts herself superbly. Let us not forget of course that she had acted in many films before being taken under the wing of Josef and had plenty of experience behind her. The difference here of course is that this was the first time that she was "The Dietrich" without her maestro, and very much a star in her own right.

Predictably charismatic and a sight to behold, she is every bit the star of the show and everything, including story, direction and set ups, is in favour of ensuring Dietrich remains striking and demanding of your attention from the first frame to her last.

Unfortunately, the film was not a commercial hit, but it did receive some good notices, and some even thought Dietrich had shifted up a gear as a screen actress. Mainly known prior to this as a figure of pure, idolised glamour, here she was playing, according to some reports, a more rounded character. The London Times observed Marlene playing "an innocent country girl. And why should she not? It is true the actress has made the vamp (the) queen of the pictures. It is true that no more glamorous, seductive, disintegrating personality ever before represented sex upon the films. Such is her range that even virginity is not beyond it." Newsweek called her "vibrant and compelling" and her performance in general as a "triumph".

She may have been playing a variant on the Dietrich idol, but she is still a highly sexualised creature in Song of Songs, something illustrated physically by the nude statue (which she actually posed for) which preserves her as a picturesque sex symbol for all time. She begins the film wide eyed, perhaps even child-like, and ends it as a woman in every way. It's a detailed, controlled effort. Importantly, the director enjoyed working with Marlene, whom he described as having a great sense of discipline. And discipline is the key word, for Dietrich, in life and on screen, committed herself totally to being the era's most seductive and desired female star. Song of Songs is another entry in her crusade through thirties cinema as the ultimate in femininity. Even Greta Garbo herself, Marlene's biggest rival at the time, was impressed by Dietrich's work in this one!

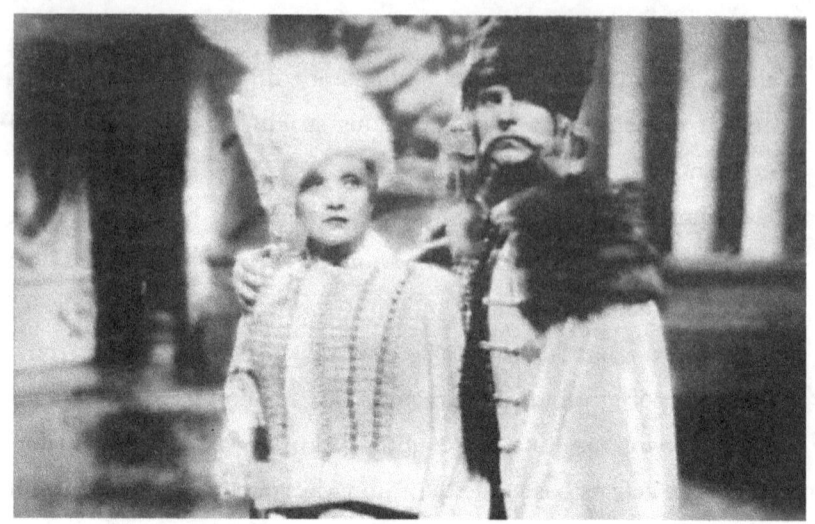

THE SCARLET EMPRESS (1934)

The last two films Marlene and Josef made together were The Scarlet Empress and The Devil is a Woman. The former, made in 1934 and featuring Dietrich as Catherine the Great, was according to von Sternberg himself, "a relentless excursion into style". Again though, this is not a case of pure style over content. Granted, the film does not pretend to be depicting the true story of Catherine the Great, and there is a level of camp here very high even for Marlene and Josef's collaborations, but there is a grace to both the film and Marlene's assured performance that fully elevates the exercise. Yes, the idea of a modern glamour figure such as Dietrich playing the powerful empress might understandably raise a titter or two, but Dietrich becomes the part, oozes pure class and embodies the hierarchal dignity of the great leader wonderfully.

At the time of release, The Scarlet Empress was often pitted against 1933's Queen Christina, featuring her so called rival Greta Garbo, but in reality von Sternberg's biopic has little in common with the earlier Garbo flick. For one, the direction is much tidier, the lighting accentuating Dietrich's wonderful features and creating a general moodiness not apparent in Queen Christina. Dietrich's performance was not a million miles from Garbo's however, and both used their European exoticism and love of suggestive sexuality to create convincing portrayals. But there really was no rivalry at all, both women clearly being above such childishness.

The Scarlet Empress charts the journey of Sophia (Dietrich), the kin of a German prince and a mother who aspires for a better life for her daughter. Sent to Russia, she marries the nephew of Empress Elizabeth, Grand Duke Peter, but becomes bored, renaming herself Catherine and amusing herself with Count Alexey Razumovsky, a womaniser who it turns out is courting the Empress. Catherine aligns herself with the Russians and when Duke Peter finds himself in power after the demise of the Empress, Catherine takes no prisoners and pushes for a reign, redubbing herself Catherine the Great, a woman who so famously rose to the top against all odds.

Of course, this being Dietrich and von Sternberg, reality comes second to fantasy and presentation. Heavily stylised, Russia becomes a backward, stunted land on the cusp of collapse, over reliant on tradition and the kind of foreboding religious imagery not present in the real Russia of the day. Still, the gargoyle screams carved in rock make for good metaphor for a land in need of a drastic change, one no doubt to be brought in by Catherine the Great. Besides, such gothic imagery is naturally perfect fodder for von Sternberg, master of shadows, mystery and dissolve.

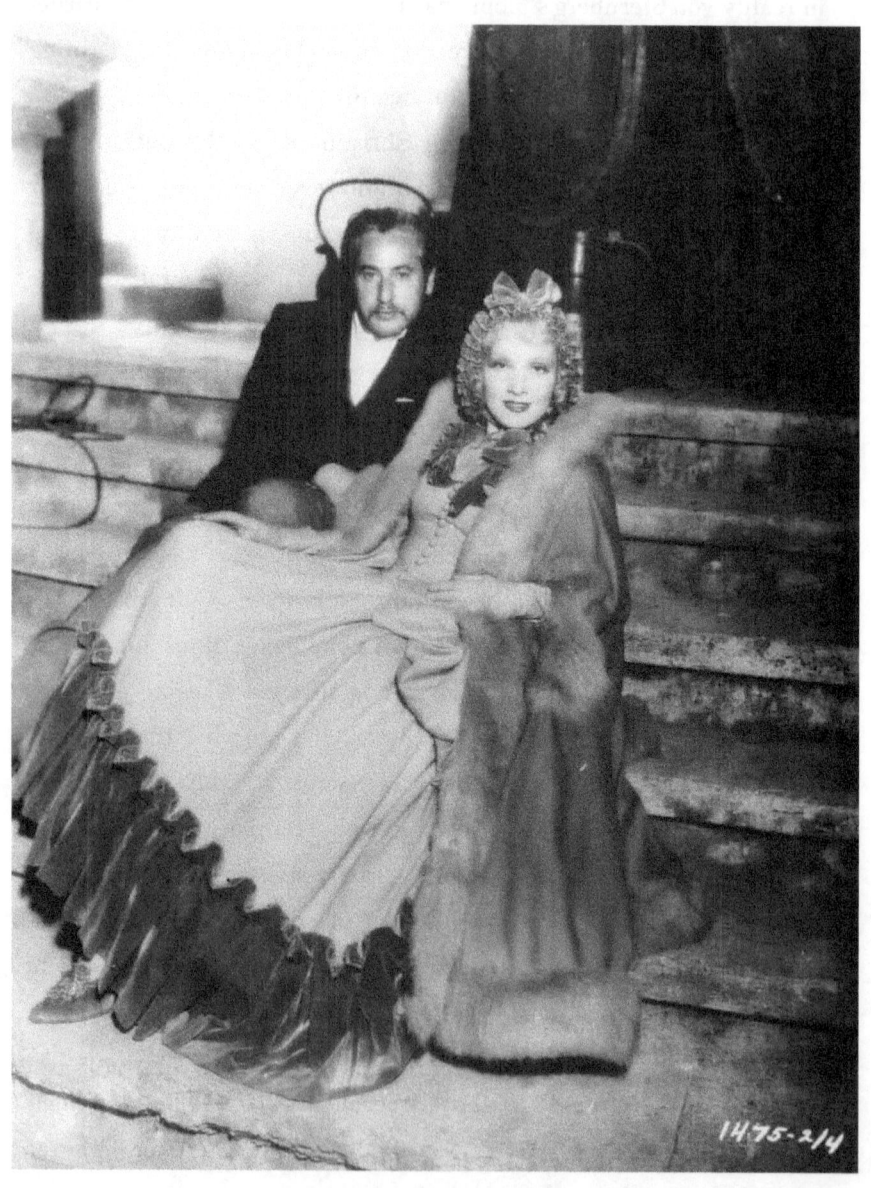

14.75-2/4

66

Dietrich herself is wonderful, dominating the film completely in a performance that is confident yet fuss free. She takes charge of the screen, reducing all the other actors to bit players who may as well be faceless. She is also at her sexiest, in a film which just before the Hollywood code came into order took advantage of the slack rules when it came to sexual suggestiveness and nudity - note the topless women being tortured and Dietrich's sex hungry performance as signs of a filmmaker running riot in a pre-prudish playground, given all the toys at his disposal.

The Scarlet Empress is viewed positively today by fans of Dietrich and von Sternberg, though some validly believe that the visuals took precedence over everything else. In his book on Marlene's films, Homer Dickens wrote, "Never before had there been such pomp and pageantry; all attention was geared to the visuals. Ferocious icons, ominous serfs, bells, cuckoo clocks, pillars, brought a Byzantine flavour to the surroundings, a kind of German expressionism."

Roger Ebert, writing a highly complimentary review of the film in 2005, agreed that there was a heck of a lot of style. "Here is a film so crammed with style, so surrounded by it and weighted down with it, that the actors peer out from the display like children in a toy store. The film tells the story of Catherine the Great as a bizarre visual extravaganza, combining twisted sexuality and bold bawdy humour as if Mel Brooks had collaborated with the Marquis de Sade. As drama, The Scarlet Empress makes no sense, nor does it attempt to. This is not a resource for history class. Its primary subject is von Sternberg's erotic obsession with Dietrich, whom he objectified in a series of movies that made her face one of the immortal icons of the cinema. Whether she could act was beside the point for him; it would have been a distraction."

Writing about Marlene's performance, Dickens saw serious flaws. "Dietrich's performance, without proper translations, was good as could be expected under the circumstances. Her earlier sequences as the shy princess were near perfect, but when she later becomes the power within the palace, there was no believability."

Ebert however, giving the film 4 out of 4 stars, raved "When Dietrich is onscreen, however, nothing is too good for her; not only do von Sternberg's lighting and cinematography make her the centre and subject of every scene, but he devises extraordinary moments for as, as when, clad in a fur uniform and cape, with an improbable sable military hat, she mounts a horse and leads a cavalry charge up the grand staircase. 'It took more than one man to change my name to Shanghai Lily,' she says in Shanghai Express, but it only took von Sternberg to make her Marlene Dietrich."

Clearly, Ebert "got" it.

THE DEVIL IS A WOMAN (1935)

"I am a teacher who took a beautiful woman, instructed her, presented her carefully," Sternberg later said, "edited her charms, disguised her imperfections and led her to crystallize a pictorial aphrodisiac. She was a perfect medium, who with intelligence absorbed my direction, and despite her own misgivings responded to my conception of a female archetype."

Their final film together came in 1935 with the romantic drama The Devil is a Woman. A cold yet expertly delivered finale for the pair, it was a fitting swan song for a duo who had made some of the most striking and memorable movies of the early talkie period. While keeping the visual purity of the silent era, Sternberg and Dietrich used sound as a tool to merely enhance the image on screen. The Devil is a Woman, in my view not one of their best collaborations, remains sharp and precise all the same, portraying Dietrich as all women and von Sternberg as every longing male.

The Devil is a Woman was made at a changing time for the film business, in particular Paramount, who had been suffering from poor profits at the box office. Seeing as von Sternberg's films were seen as expensive extravagances, Paramount were only willing to indulge the filmmaker for so long. Proud for some time to be releasing films that offered more than standard thrills, Paramount drew the line at films that made them little profit. Unfortunately, once The Devil is a Woman was released to little fan fare and underwhelming box office, his contract was finished. After seven films, it seemed as if the public had fallen out of love with Dietrich and von Sternberg's eccentric, stylised movies. Some reviewers however were still won over, with

The New York Times calling it their best film together since The Blue Angel, though most found it lacklustre.

Variety however simply had to praise Dietrich. "Not even Garbo in the Orient has approached, for spectacular effects, Dietrich in Spain. Her costumes are completely incredible, but completely fascinating and suitable to The Devil is a Woman. They reek with glamour. Miss Dietrich emerges as a glorious achievement, a supreme consolidation of the sartorial, make-up and photographic arts."

Their relationship as filmmaker and star had begun with a bang, but ended with a whimper. The truth is though, that The Devil is a Woman has stood the test of time. It has little of the distracting subplots of their earlier films and is certainly more straight forward, if not harsher. This is not a schmaltzy parting of the ways, but a no nonsense split, a master of cinema bidding farewell to his beautiful muse through visual metaphors, his feeling veiled by cinematic stylisation. There is no moral message, no real heart to the picture, which could not have been more apt for a von Sternberg aware that the pair had run their course as a unit. "Dietrich and I have progressed as far as possible together, and my being with her will help neither her nor me," he said bluntly.

The unsettling part of the film is the fact that the two male leads look remarkably like Josef himself. When Alexander Walker brought this point up in an interview with von Sternberg, the director replied "Everyone in my films is like me... spiritually." Was The Devil is a Woman, with its von Sternberg doppelganger romantic lead, smooching passionately with Dietrich, his way of self inflicting a last masochistic punch in the gut?

Few at the time mourned the end of this collaboration, with Dietrich getting through a commercial down spell before regaining momentum as a screen star within a year or two. Sternberg though, was a little bitter, and displayed true arrogance when he later said, "No puppet in the history of the world has been submitted to as much manipulation as a leading lady of mine who, in seven films, not only had hinges and voice under control other than her own but the expression of her eyes and the nature of her thoughts." He later also observed, "Miss Dietrich is me - I am Miss Dietrich!" Though his point is valid, and he very much did carve Dietrich into the woman he desired her to be, he too would have had nothing without her. To say he even led the way Dietrich thought may have been an overstatement, but von Sternberg was in part living out his own fantasy as puppet master in real life as well as on screen. He may have been slightly deluded or prone to overstating his egomaniacal power over Marlene, but it's a fact they both gained much from one another. It could also be said though that with Dietrich's exit von Sternberg lost much more than a mere puppet, but his livelihood, his commercial appeal and, perhaps worst of all, his muse.

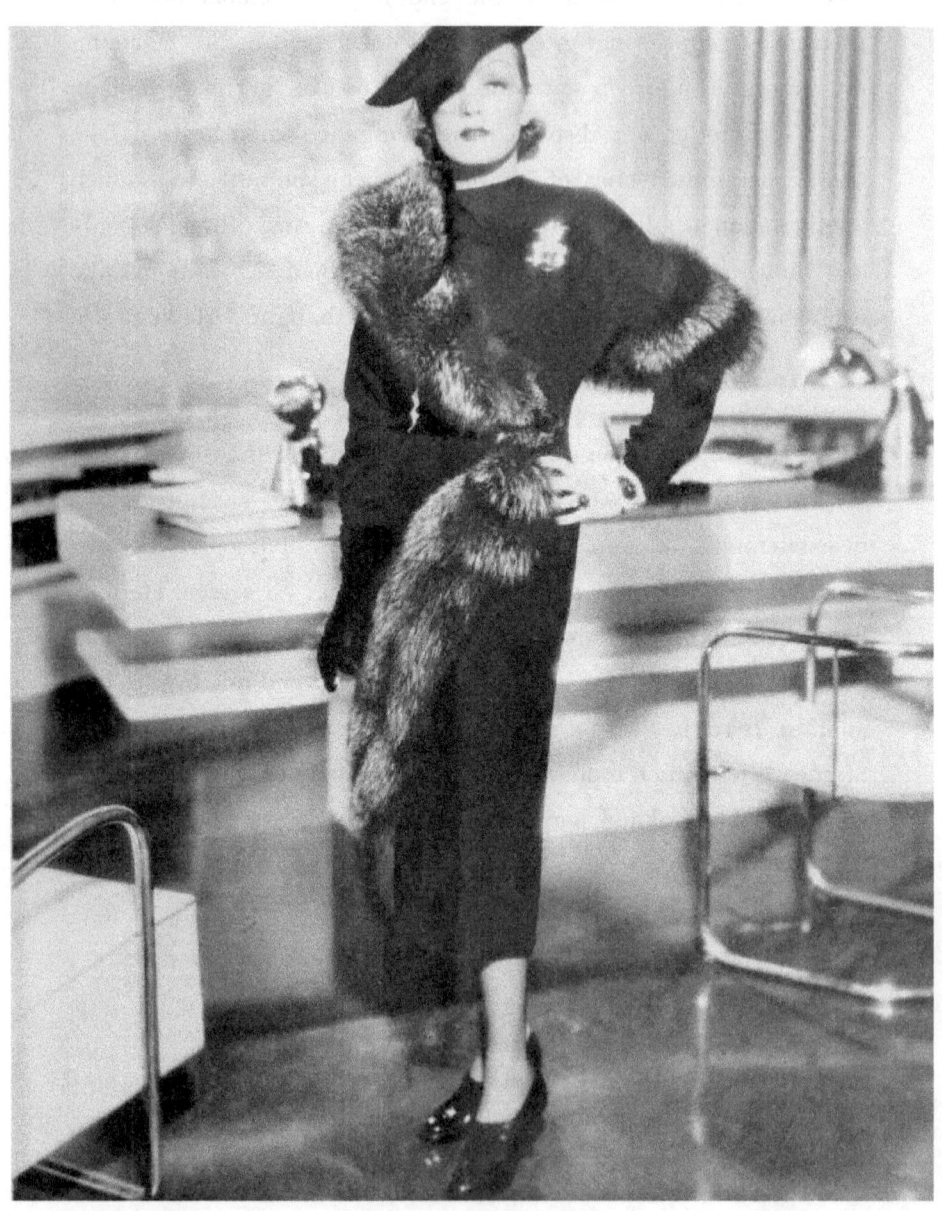

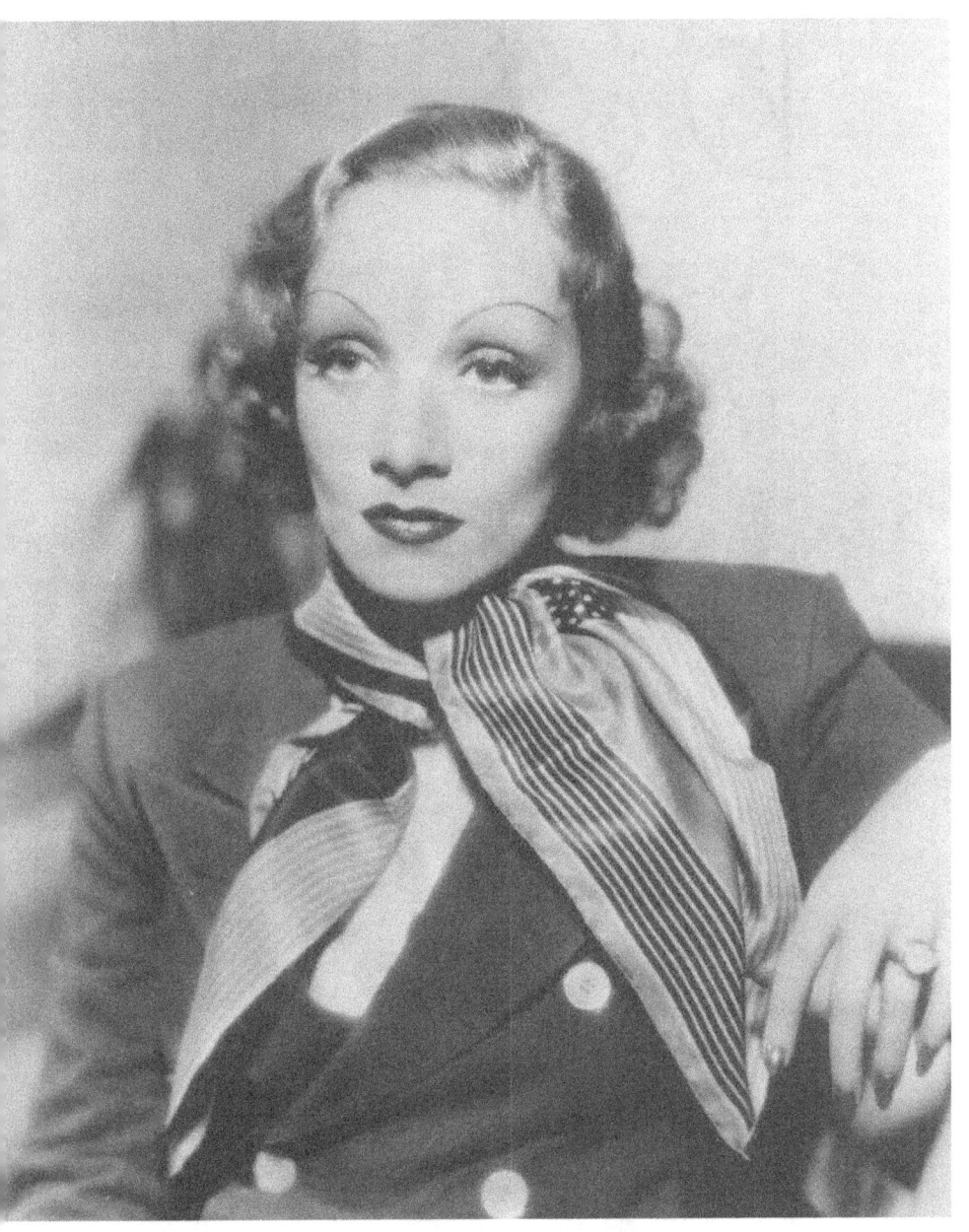

"DESIRE"

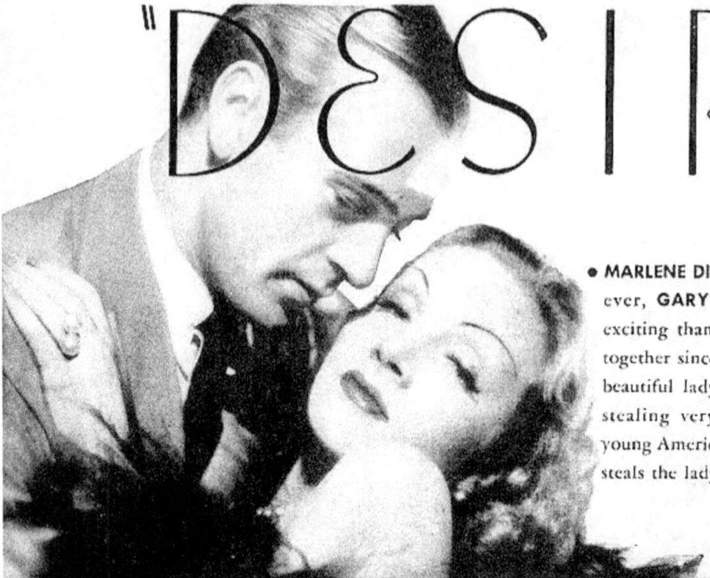

• **MARLENE DIETRICH**, more alluring than ever, **GARY COOPER**, more casually exciting than ever, in their first picture together since *Morocco* ... a yarn about a beautiful lady with a very bad habit of stealing very expensive jewels and a young American motor car engineer who steals the lady's heart.

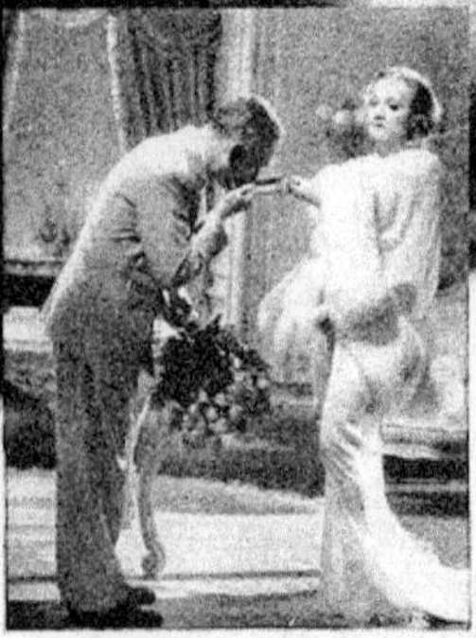

Just an old European custom ... but we'd like to be John Halliday, the gentleman who's doing the hand kissing.

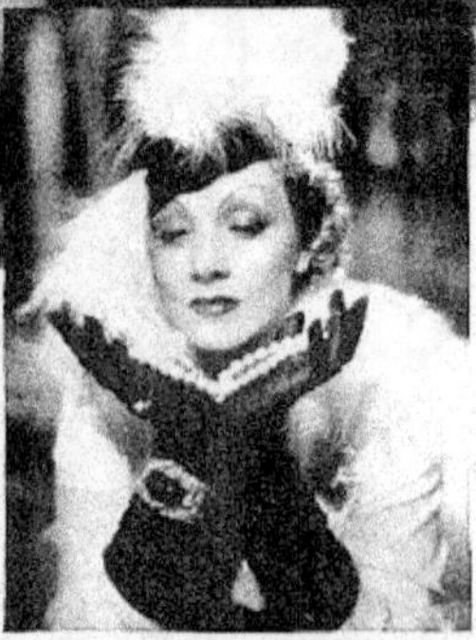

Marlene seems to be going in for jewels in a big way ... also note the pom-pom hat. It'll set a style.

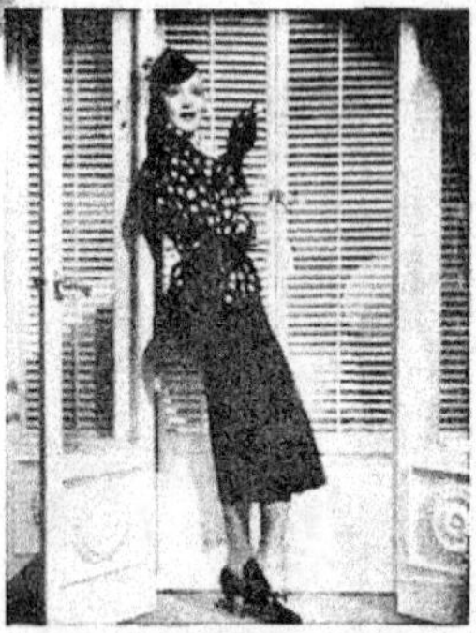

This ought to be in color, for those star like spots in the crisp black taffeta jacket are a really ravishing shade of pink.

...A Paramount Picture Directed by Frank Borzage from a comedy by Hans Szekely and R. A. Stemmle.

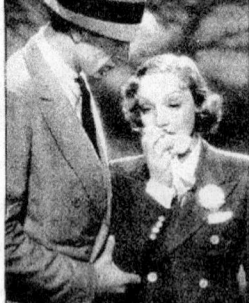

This shot is from the picture. Gary apparently has said something pretty tough, for that's a real handkerchief and those are real tears.

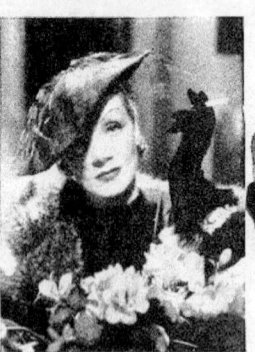

Marlene shows she's still loyal to the beret, this time, a novel black antelope affair, designed by Travis Banton Paramount's Fashion Expert.

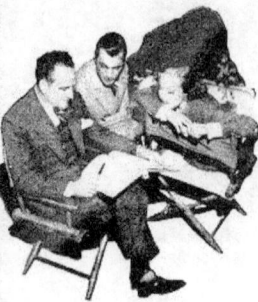

Frank Borzage talks over a scene from "Desire" with Marlene and Gary.

DESIRE (1936)

Dietrich spent some time in late 1935 filming I Loved A Soldier with Henry Hathaway, only to see the film abandoned mid way through production. In 1938, Hathaway gave it another go, cast new actors and finished it under a different title. Though 1936 didn't go as planned, Dietrich did make one of her best pictures that year with Desire, a film she often called her personal favourite, or more to the point the only film she need not be ashamed of. Away from von Sternberg, she was flourishing nicely.

Desire was directed and produced by Frank Borzage and was a remake of a 1933 German film called Happy Days in Aranjuez. Co-producer Ernst Lubitsch assigned a trio of screenwriters to carve a story that would bring out the best in Dietrich physically and as an actress. Lubitsch made the wise decision of teaming her once again with Gary Cooper, who had set sparks flying with Marlene in the 1930 classic Morocco, perhaps in a bid to make Dietrich feel safe in the absence of her former maestro. It worked and Marlene later said she felt secure with both her co star and the producer.

The story concerns Dietrich as Madeleine, a jewel thief who begins the film conning a jeweller named Aristide (Ernest Cossart) and Maurice the psychiatrist (Alan Mowbray) by telling each man she is wed to the other. Her plan pays off when Aristride sends millions of francs worth of pearls to the shrink's office expecting a payment, which Dietrich slyly makes off with after introducing the two stooges. When she flees, she runs across Gary Cooper as an American engineer named Tom, who fixes problems with her car and ends up having the pearls hidden in his coat pocket by a scheming Dietrich.

When the jacket gets mixed up, she finds her plan going seriously awry, and after adopting the guise of a baroness, proceedings become more muddled and farcical.

Looking back on her career years later, Marlene singled Desire out for praise... though it was the faintest imaginable. "The only film I need not be ashamed of is Desire, directed by Frank Borzage and based on a script by Ernst Lubitsch. I found Gary Cooper a little less monosyllabic than before. He was finally rid of Lupe Vélez, who had been at his heels constantly throughout the shooting of Morocco. Desire became a good film and, moreover, also proved to be a box-office success. The script was excellent, the roles superb - one more proof that these elements are more important than actors."

With that last statement, Dietrich was belittling her own importance, not only in the history of film but within each picture she made. Yes, script was vital to the success of her movies, but without her in the lead roles the films, though presumably still effective, would have lost much in her absence. Desire is a case in point; a finely constructed and directed picture, it undoubtedly still relies on Marlene's magnetism. A lighter role, less fetishised than her von Sternberg roles, Dietrich is here given room to breathe, flesh out her character beyond limitations and make her more believable, at least in the rather far fetched and typically Hollywood-ised proceedings.

Reviews at the time noted a shift in Dietrich's performance. The New York Times said that producer Lubitsch had "freed Marlene from Josef von Sternberg's artistic bondage and has brought her vibrantly alive in Desire. Permitted to walk, breathe, smile and shrug as a human being instead of a canvas for the Louvre, Miss Dietrich recaptures some of the freshness and gayety of spirit that was hers in The Blue Angel..."

Indeed, one does feel a link between Desire and The Blue Angel, though not in their plots but in the light they depict the great Dietrich. Separated by six years and a host of iconic, unforgettable though highly stylised roles for von Sternberg, the Dietrich of Desire is like Lola-Lola in that she is liberated and not confined to a choreographed setting. There is more space here for Dietrich to be playful, something she certainly wasn't when being the living embodiment of von Sternberg's desires in their pictures together. Here is a more human Dietrich, less work of art and more relatable character.

Writing in The Spectator, Graham Greene said Desire was "the best film in which Miss Marlene Dietrich has appeared since she left Germany, and the most amusing new film to be seen in London this week." He had a point. But Marlene aside, it's beautifully directed and the script is sharp and carefully worked out. Cooper is good, but he is merely there it seems to work off the dynamic and wonderful Dietrich. Desire is a great slice of 1930s Hollywood escapism, and while Dietrich was certainly wrong when saying it was the only film she need not be ashamed of, it certainly is one of her finest and most lasting movies from this rich and golden period.

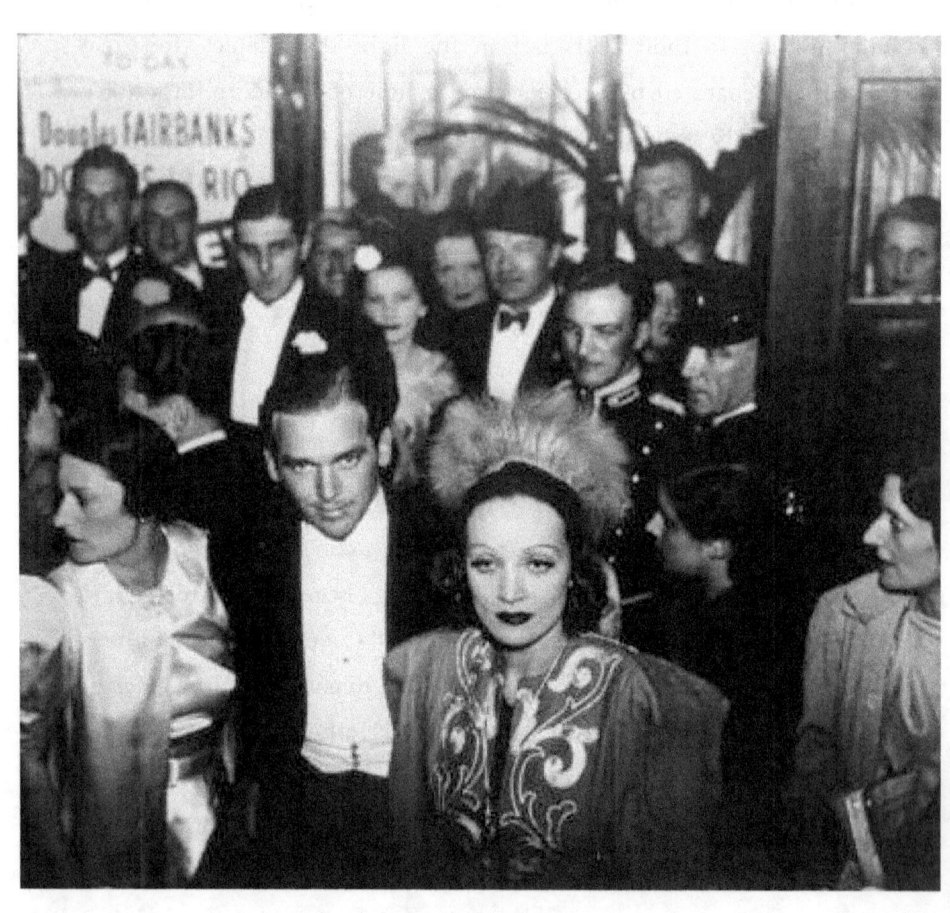

With Douglas Fairbanks Jr in 1936

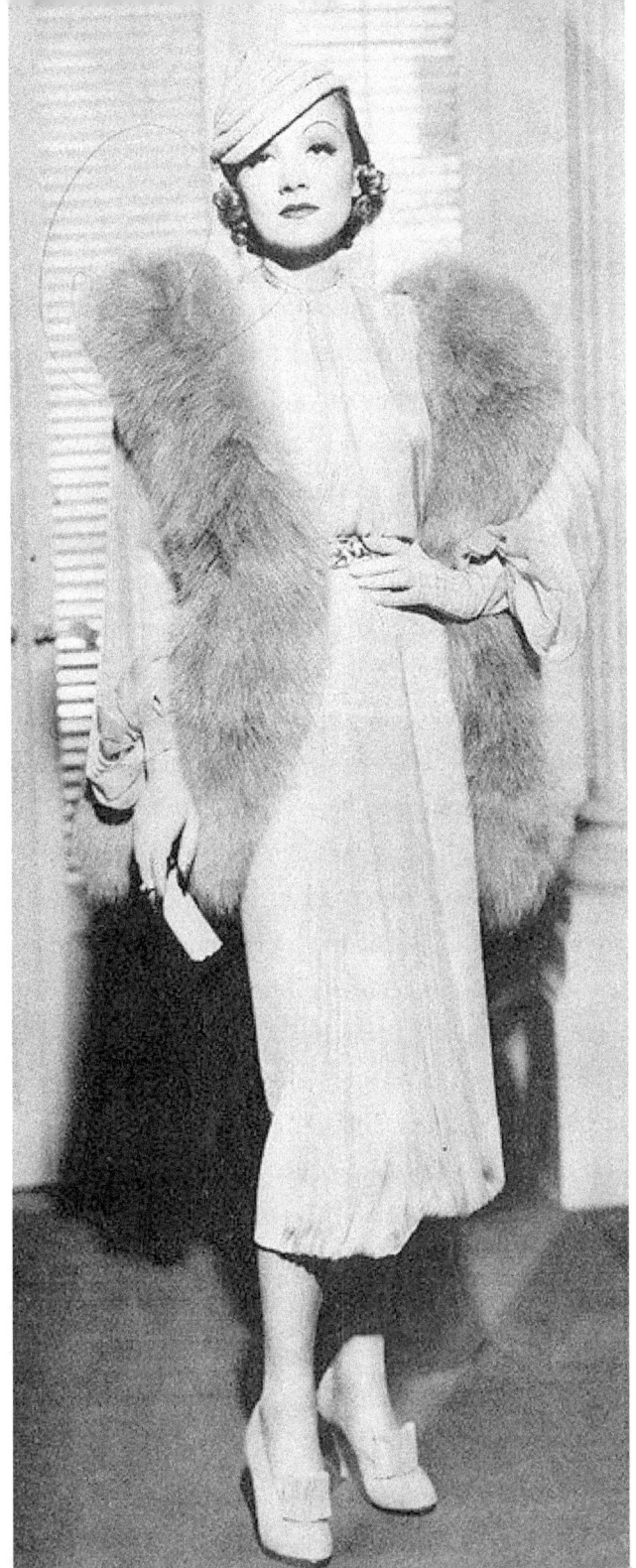

THE GARDEN OF ALLAH (1936)

With 1936's The Garden of Allah, Marlene Dietrich appeared for the first time, in all her glory, in colour film. The third movie to be filmed in Three-strip Technicolor, it was technically a very important step forwards for the industry, with the cinematographers being rewarded Oscars for their work. However, the main reason most people were going to come and see The Garden of Allah was not for its dazzling colour (though that too was a big draw), but for Marlene.

Charles Boyer stars as Boris, a monk who flees his monastery just as Domini Enfilden (Dietrich), a rich heir, leaves home after caring for her recently dead father. They both end up in the deserts of North Africa and, as one would expect, fall in love. Once married, they go on a honeymoon to a far away desert, but when they come across a group of French legionnaires, Boris's true identity and past as a monk is revealed once the troops taste the liqueur he makes them, the recipe of which belongs solely to his old monastery. Will his wife accept his past and the fact he has gone against the Lord and broken his sacred vows, or is this act of deception too much to bare?

Dietrich had sent hearts fluttering in the desert before, in the iconic Morocco, and here she was, once again, an exotic creature in an exotic location, only of a totally different kind. This time she was in colour, radiating majestically amidst the rainbow of shades around her. Of course, this being an early colour picture, the production got over excited and adorned the cast with often garishly coloured costumes. But all this exuberance works, adding flavour to the rather camp surroundings. It also brings out Dietrich's beauty, perhaps even more than black and white did, if that were possible.

The plot is engaging and the cast, particularly Boyer, do well in their roles, but once again, as expected, the film belongs to Dietrich. Actually giving a balanced and grounded performance, she is infinitely watchable, as striking as ever but more effervescent in full, deep colour. Her very first appearance in the film, for me at least, remains one of the best moments in Dietrich's filmography. At the convent, a nun converses with a group of children. She pulls back a beautiful stain glass window to reveal a divine, almost heavenly Dietrich, on her knees at the feet of a religious monument, surrounded by candles as she preys under her breath. The scene sets her up as the woman who gave everything up to care for her dad, only to be heartbroken by his death. This is Dietrich as martyr, a holy figure far removed from her idealised stance when under the direction of von Sternberg. Here she is selfless, even wholesome at times, and thoroughly decent, committed to faith and the discipline and respect which comes with its strict dedication.

As a characterisation, I believe this was the best work Dietrich had done up to this date, in one picture going from sensual pin up to serious actress. Some reviews however did not see it this way. Herald Tribune complained she was "still a monosyllabic clothes-horse", definitely an unfair appraisal when viewing her well rounded portrayal of Domini. Others however, like The Literary Digest, said it was the best performance of her career so far.

Today, The Garden of Allah is unfairly overlooked, though true fans of Dietrich rate it highly. (Dietrich herself called it, on set, "trash".) For me it is definitely one of her finest films and especially her strongest performances, a bold and rich example of early colour pictures at their most vibrant.

KNIGHT WITHOUR ARMOUR (1937)

Marlene Dietrich then journeyed across seas, and got the typical star treatment, to make a film in the UK. Though an English production (one distributed by United Artists), Knight Without Armour was directed by the Belgian actor and filmmaker Jacques Feyder, based on James Hilton's book with a screenplay by an American (Frances Marion) and a Hungarian (Lajos Biro). A multi cultural affair, it featured a German in the lead with English Robert Donat as the co-star and male lead.

Donat plays A.J. Fothergill, a young man assigned to spy on Russia on behalf of Britain, who first gains access to a revolutionary group who plan to kill General Vladinoff, whose daughter just happens to be Marlene Dietrich, terrific as Alexandra. When the plot fails, Fothergill is sent to Siberia. As the First World War rages on, Alexandra is widowed and taken prisoner due to her aristocratic background. It is up to Fothergill, under the guise of Peter Ouranoff, to save the beautiful doomed woman, though he did not bet on falling in love with her.

This rather odd, often disjointed film is certainly not one of Dietrich's finest moments from her glory years, but it is engaging and at times sharp in its various plot shifts. Donat does a good job, though due to a week long comedown with asthma, producer Alexander Korda did consider replacing him. Dietrich, however, saved Donat the sack and insisted they wait for his recovery. The film, a fairly lower budget production for Dietrich (especially in comparison to what she'd been used to with von Sternberg), gets by on decent acting and a script which, though overly fussy at times, keeps you caring about the plight of the characters until the very end.

Dietrich herself is, once again, a class act, delivering a star turn and genuinely coming across as something quite extraordinary. That's not to say this is a complex or effective performance on a technical level, but it is Dietrich at her eye catching best. She was supposed to have been paid a reported $250,000 for her part and a 10 percent of whatever profit the picture made. When the budget swelled to $350,000, Korda regretfully told Dietrich she couldn't possibly be given her due amount. Marlene, to her credit, accepted this on the grounds that Korda let her old director friend, Josef von Sternberg, direct his upcoming I, Claudius. (Korda did so, but the film was never finished.)

Reviews were not overly enthusiastic. Variety complained it was "A laboured effort to keep this picture neutral on the subject of the Russian Revolution finally completely overshadows the simple love story intertwining Marlene Dietrich and Robert Donat." Slightly more positive was the observation that "Performances on the whole are good, though Dietrich restricts herself to just looking glamorous in any setting or costume."

ANGEL (1937)

German filmmaker Ernst Lubitsch stepped forward to helm Dietrich's next feature, producing and directing 1937's Angel. Adapted from Melchoir Lengyel's novel by Guy Bolton and Russell Medcraft, it was another lavish, exuberant outing for Marlene. Angel concerns a plot revolving around a love triangle between Dietrich as Lady Maria Barker, the disregarded wife of Sir Frederick (Herbert Marshall) and India based Anthony Halton (Melvyn Douglas). During their brief romance, Halton dubs her "angel", but she insists no one learns of their liaison and leaves suddenly without a goodbye. Halton, so smitten with Lady Maria, sets out to find her at any cost.

Like Desire, Angel gave Marlene the chance to lighten her load and play in less portentous surroundings. That said, the film lacks the magnitude of her work with Josef von Sternberg, not to mention the atmosphere and irresistible camp pomp. The story is engaging enough, but in some ways it feels a little laboured. Dietrich herself is watchable as ever, adorned in glorious costumes and radiating charisma and style every step of the way, yet the movie never really lifts off. Granted, it's a very old fashioned film and certainly one of its time, but considering the other work she did in the thirties, it's rather limp in comparison.

The film does have its merits, Marlene's presence aside. Though the leads lack character and fail to measure up to Dietrich's statue-esque, awe inspiring presence, credit must go to Charles Lang's cinematography and the music score by Frederick Hollander. Otherwise, Angel could well be the weakest of the movies she made in the golden era of Hollywood.

Reviews were not enthusiastic. The New York Times' Frank Nugent was hardly won over by the star, and in fact saw her very presence as the film's main problem. He complained, "Unfortunately, Miss Dietrich is at the root of (the film's) evils. She still is a lovely lady, glamorously gowned, but she has the unhappy gift of absorbing the camera's attention to the exclusion of the other members of her company. The film comes to a full stop every time she raises or lowers the artificially elongated Dietrich eyelids. After looking deeply into the liquid hollows of her eyes, we begin to agree with Schopenhauer that women are sphinxes without riddles."

Time Out, writing more recently it has to be said, commented: "To the less committed, Dietrich - caressingly photographed by Charles Lang in a manner that doesn't quite make the Sternberg grade - bats her eyelashes once too often and twice too coyly."

The truth is that Angel is far from being Dietrich's best work. Performance-wise she is fine, but her role and grasp of it fail to set off the sparks she so elegantly ignited when under the wings of von Sternberg. As a silly pot boiler however, it is hardly the worst thing you could watch. If not for Dietrich though, it is doubtful whether anyone, myself included, would bother to the take time out to view it.

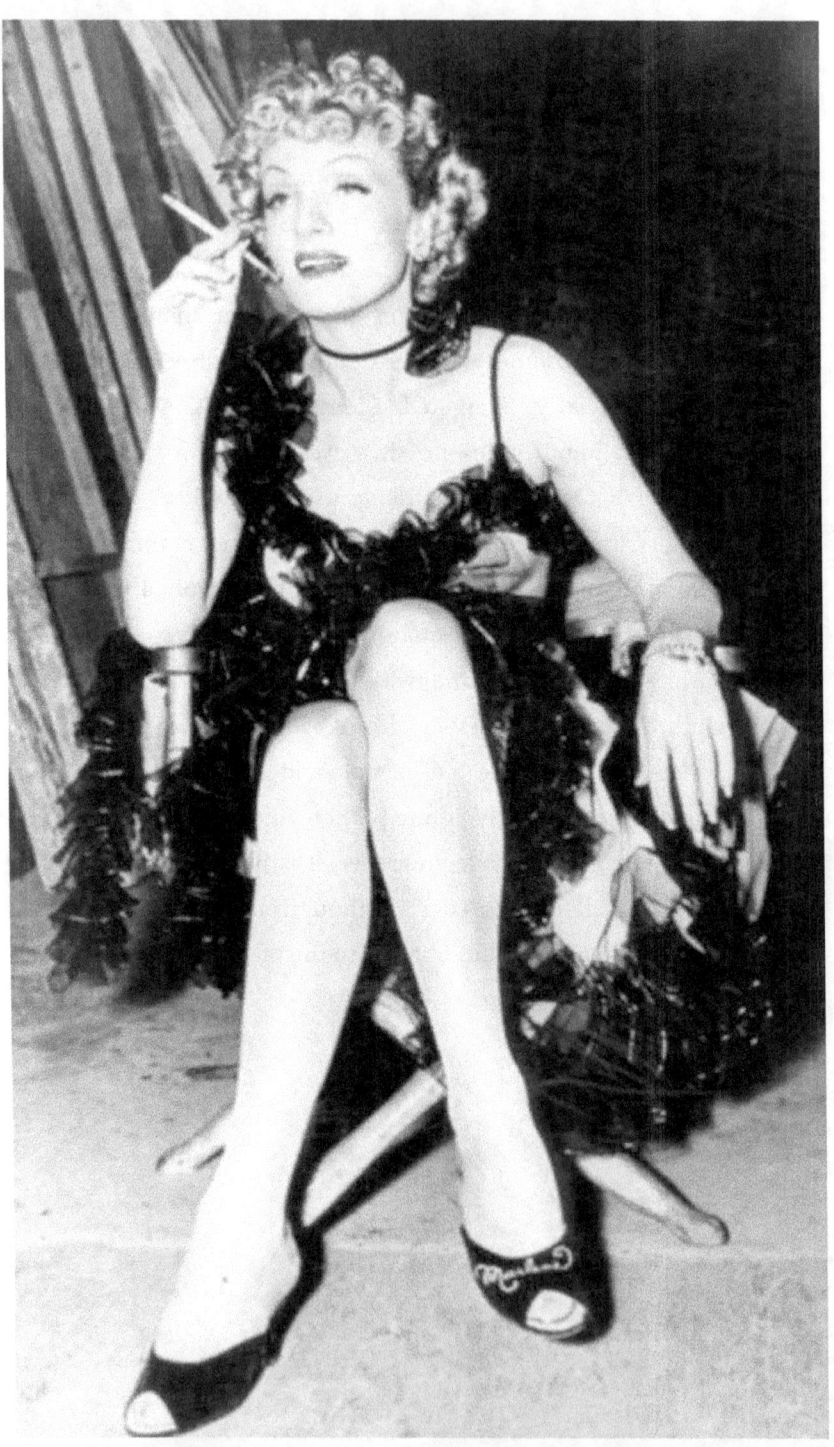

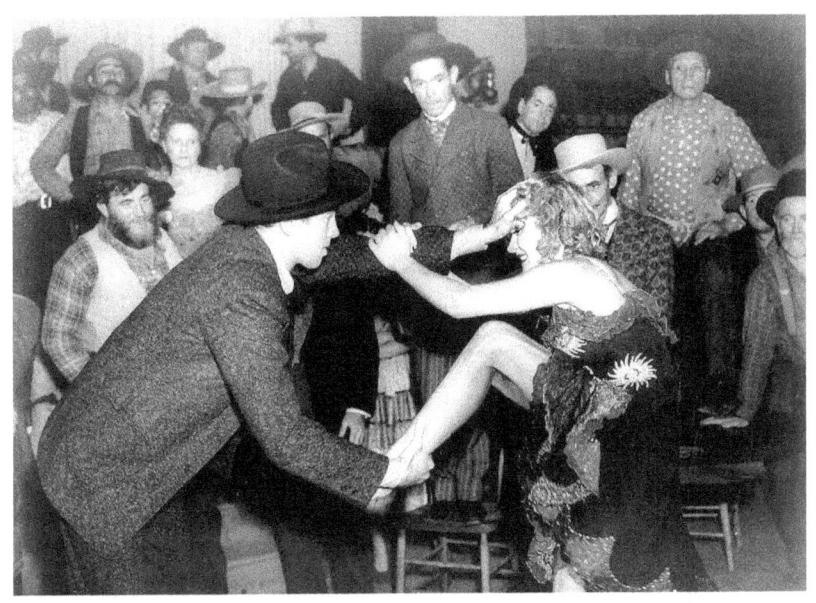

DESTRY RIDES AGAIN (1939)

Destry Rides Again was the funniest, liveliest and most outrageous film Marlene Dietrich ever appeared in. Today it's a vital part of her myth, as important to her legend as Shanghai Lily or the gender bending temptress of Morocco. In George Marshall's spoof western, set in an obscure small town called Bottleneck, she's Frenchy, the sexy, sultry saloon singer who, with her bar-owner boyfriend Kent, has a hold over cattle ranchers. The mayor, as crooked as can be, hires the town drunkard to be the sheriff, ensuring advantages can be continued to be taken under his loose, inebriated regime. When Deputy Dimsdale sniffs out the town's problems, he hires Tom Destry Jr (James Stewart) to straighten out the place and its increasingly wild inhabitants. Given his approach leans more towards the communicative than the forceful, Destry is at first a joke to the people of Bottleneck, though as he toughens up he does eventually gain some appreciation and respect.

By the time Destry Rides Again came about, Dietrich was considered to be at her lowest commercial state, even dubbed "box office poison" by insiders. Opting out of Hollywood, she visited Europe and planned to make a film in Paris, though it never came to fruition. While over seas, producer Joe Pasternak called her offering the Frenchy role in his latest western, along with a reduced fee of $70,000. Though hesitant to accept such a small (!) pay check, Dietrich knew she had to take the chance. Thankfully it paid off. The film proved a sizeable commercial hit and re-established her as a movie star and a box office winner.

Though it seems odd to say so, given she was only nine years into her career as a Hollywood star, Destry Rides Again was very much her second rising, her big comeback after a few lacklustre, underwhelming pictures. Established firmly as the most exciting and seductive siren of the early thirties, those days of stylised glory in the likes of The Blue Angel, Dishonoured and Shanghai Express seemed so long ago after the muted receptions of her more recent pictures. With Destry Rides Again however, giving a charismatic, magnetic and hugely entertaining performance, Dietrich was at her peak yet again. She had already proven her skill at being every man's fantasy - effectively a walking work of art for her director - and now here she was, the new queen of comedy in the old Wild West, an unlikely turnaround if there ever was one.

She has some wonderful moments in the film. Her fight with Una Merkel is certainly memorable, and in its day attracted the attention of the censors. And Dietrich also enjoys a rowdy bar room brawl with

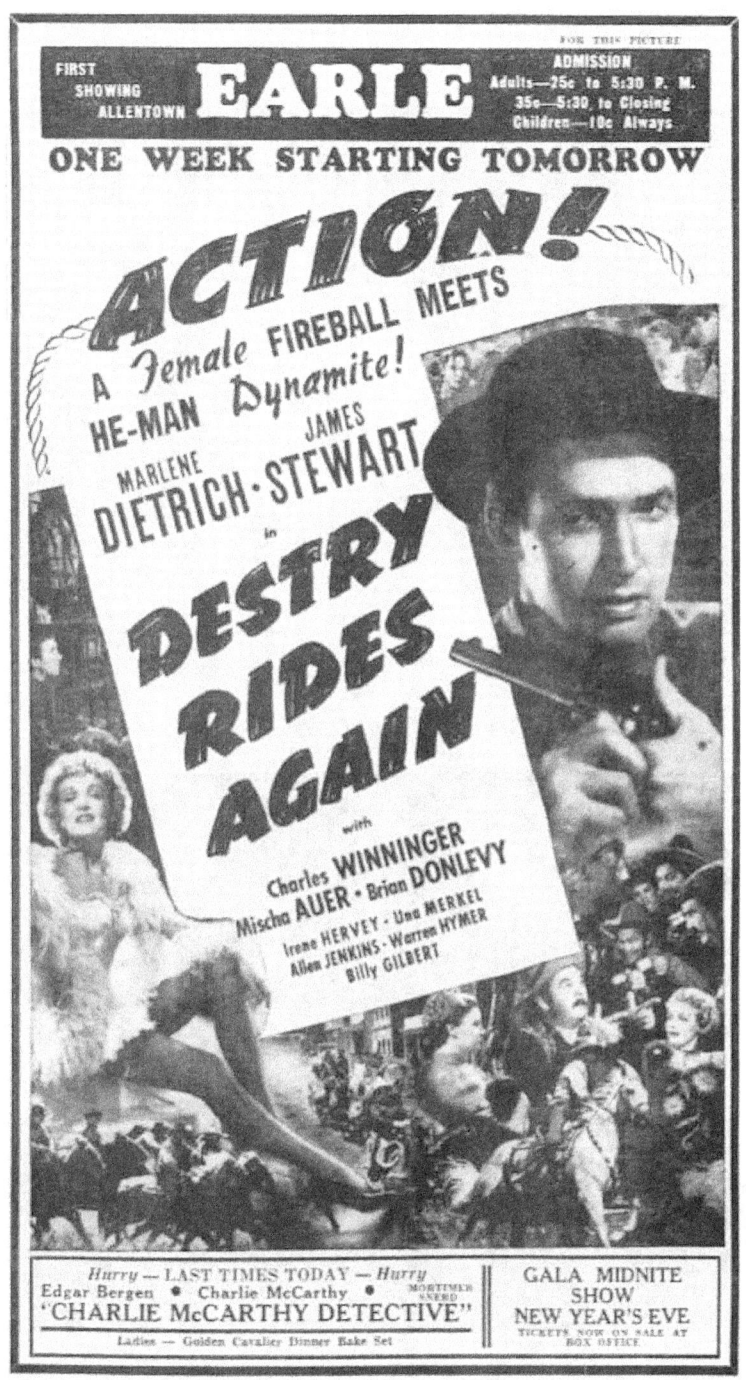

89

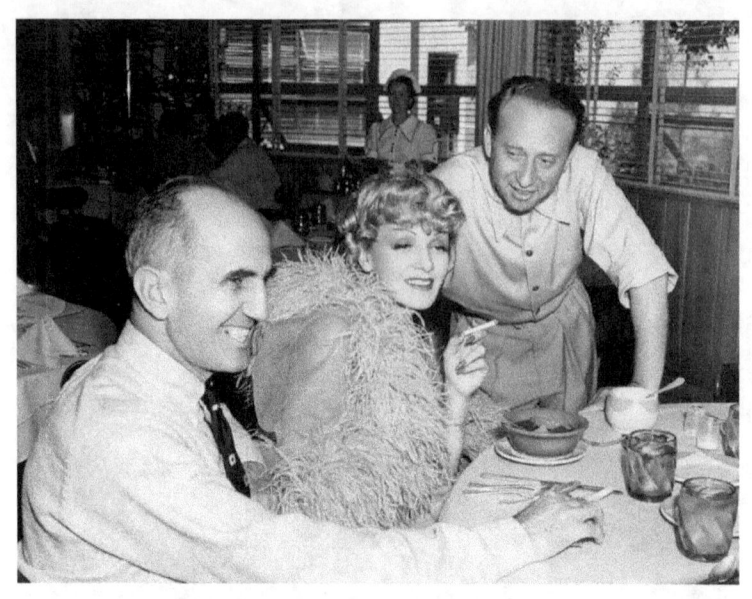

Dietrich as Frenchy in Destry Rides Again

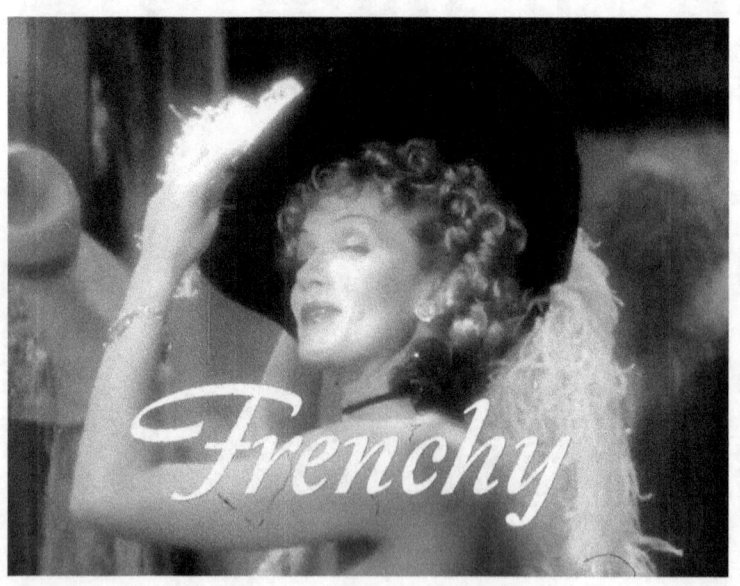

James Stewart, a hilarious moment in which Marlene soars. James Stewart later recalled she was really throwing those bottles and chairs hard, and that he narrowly escaped injury. (It's been reported that Dietrich and Stewart enjoyed an affair during the making of the film, perhaps explaining the dynamic chemistry they share together.)

Other than earning good box office and setting Marlene back up as a force to be reckoned with - not merely a face from the past - it was also popular with critics. The New York Times commended the casting of Dietrich, complimenting her success in a role that was drastically different from the ones that had made her famous. Variety wrote that "Destry Rides Again is anything but a super-western. It's just plain, good entertainment, primed with action and laughs and human sentiment."

Retrospectively Destry Rides Again has gained a healthy reputation in the comic western genre, not to mention within Dietrich's own varied oeuvre. While she directly inspired Madeline Khan's Lily Von Shtupp in Mel Brooks' Blazing Saddles, Dietrich's Frenchy became iconic in her own right. The picture is hard to fault, and everyone, even down to the bit parters, is perfect in their roles. Stewart would go on to sharpen his acting skills in many a classic after this, and would become a western staple. Dietrich would see it as a landmark film, proving the public could accept her outside von Sternberg's grip. Here she was full of vigour and energy, von Sternberg's painting come to life before our eyes.

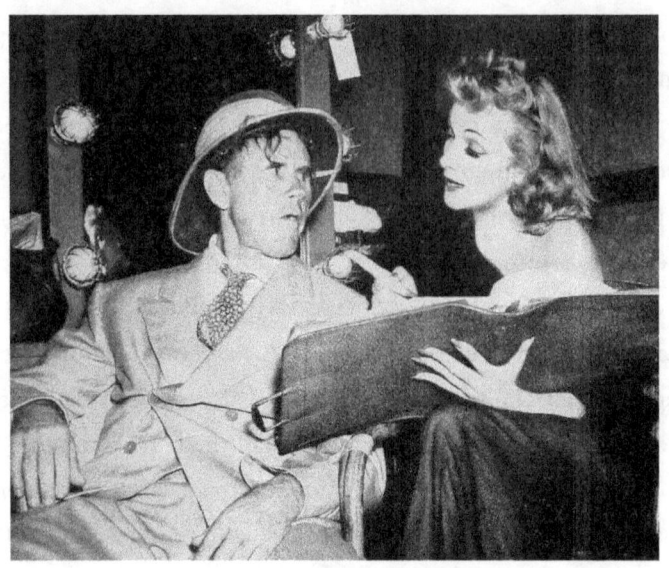

SEVEN SINNERS (1940)

Hot off the roaring success of Destry rides Again, Dietrich bounced straight back up with a film called Seven Sinners. Directed by Tay Garnett (pictured above on set with Marlene), it paired Dietrich for the first time with John Wayne, with whom she would make three pictures in all. Dietrich accepted the role for $150,000, double the fee she received for Destry Rides Again, though one could say that considering the success of her preceding picture, the pay rise was deserved. It has been reported that Dietrich urged the producer, Joe Pasternak, to cast John Wayne, who typically said after her first sighting of him, "Mama wants that for Christmas!" (Wayne famously relented Dietrich's advances, though they were friendly with one another.)

Seven Sinners stars Dietrich as singer Bijou Blanche, whose risqué career has seen her banned from all the South Sea Islands. Broderick

Crawford stars as Edward, an AWOL navy officer, while Mischa Auer is a pick pocket and magician. John Wayne enters the plot as the dashing Naval Lieutenant Dan Brent, and Bijou begins to fall in love. But will they, and indeed can they, stay together?

Seven Sinners could be seen as a direct follow up to Destry. Of course, Dietrich plays a different role, but it had a similar tone, some of the same cast and also, like Destry, featured the music of Frank Skinner, here working with Hans Salter. The pay out gamble paid off and Seven Sinners became a success for the studio. Even today, it is seen as one of the finer Dietrich films of the 1940s and onwards. She is terrific in the film, dynamic and arresting throughout. Her rendition of the song I've Been in Love Before is sublime and worth the price of the film alone. That said, the picture looks brilliant, has a lively script, is wonderfully directed and features a top notch cast all at their best. Still, it is Dietrich's show through and through, and her spoofy performance is among her finest characterisations. Whereas Frenchy was a wild and manic creation, it is a mere caricature in comparison to the part she crafts here. Indeed, Bijou is one of the most memorable faces from Dietrich's legendary gallery.

Writing at the time of release, New York Herald Tribune claimed she was even better in Seven Sinners than she had in her breakthrough film, The Blue Angel. Whether that is true or not is, of course, down to opinion, but Dietrich had certainly evolved and developed in the ten years which separated her latest hit from her Hollywood debut. Development and progress was rare in Hollywood, but Marlene was ageing like a fine wine and only getting better.

THE FLAME OF NEW ORLEANS (1941)

Marlene Dietrich worked for producer Joe Pasternak the third and final time with 1941's The Flame of New Orleans, an enjoyable comedy drama with Dietrich once again giving it her all. Rene Clair was assigned to direct Dietrich's latest picture, which cast her as Claire Ledeux, a woman who mysteriously vanishes on the day of her wedding and whose dress is found floating in a river. Told in flashback, the details of Claire's life are revealed as the enigmatic tale begins to unravel.

The Flame of New Orleans was in development for quite a while, and after back and forth fussing and casting issues, filming finally began in January of 1941. Dietrich, very much the new darling of Universal, did not get along with her co star Bruce Cabot. She later dubbed him "an awfully stupid actor, unable to remember his lines or cues. Cabot was very conceited. He wouldn't accept any help. I finally resigned myself to paying for his lessons, so that he would at least know his lines."

There were other issues too. Screenwriter Norman Krasna also got on the wrong side of Marlene when he said she was useless at comedy, commenting on her stiff, frozen face. Despite these issues, no one was re-cast at the last minute, Clair retained his professionalism and the film wrapped efficiently.

Pasternak later said The Flame of New Orleans was perhaps the most interesting of the three pictures he and Dietrich made together. I disagree. It is engaging in its own right but comes nowhere near the dynamism of Destry Rides Again and Seven Sinners. Granted, it is a very different film, but Dietrich's grasp of the role is not as firm, and her co stars, it has to be said, are not quite up for the task of standing opposite the great Dietrich. The film certainly looks beautiful, and Dietrich is as hypnotically watchable as ever, but the film fails to soar at any point.

Reviews were OK, but it was clear that the momentum from Dietrich's two preceding pictures had dimmed somewhat. Many criticised Clair's direction (the infamous film writer Hedda Hopper said it lacked the zip she demanded) while others questioned Dietrich's comedic skills.... or lack of them. Clair himself later commented, "The critics were most cruel to Dietrich, chiding her for being mannered again and all the rest of it. She thought she was spoofing her old self, but apparently the gentle satire was lost."

Dietrich said the film "was a flop. I played a double role and, as always, wore lavish costumes, but that wasn't enough. I didn't particularly like Clair, but I didn't hate him as much as the rest did."

The Flame of New Orleans was a commercial disappointment, putting a dint in Dietrich's run of box office success. Today it is often disregarded - quite rightly I might add - as minor Marlene. The Radio Times, writing retrospectively, saw major problems with Dietrich's performance, writing "This twist on the old gold-digger formula offers only middling entertainment, and shows just how ordinary Dietrich could be and how she needed rather more appealing leading men than Young and Cabot."

A valiant effort, The Flame of New Orleans was something of a misfire, an unfortunate bump in the road just when Dietrich was picking up speed.

MANPOWER (1941)

The same year she starred in the rather disappointing The Flame of New Orleans, Dietrich was over at Warner Brothers making Manpower, a stylish film noir thriller directed by Raoul Walsh. Unlike her rather misguided and miscast picture with Rene Clair, Manpower was a commercial hit all over the world, turning a good profit for the studio. It no doubt helped that Dietrich was at ease during production, mainly because she was cast alongside George Raft and Edward G Robinson, both of whom were long time firm friends of hers. Funnily enough, the film gained some press notice during filming, when Robinson and Raft got into an on-set fist fight. Still, the pair got over their differences and the film was shot on time and within budget.

Robinson plays Hank McHenry, a power line engineer who works as a foreman after getting injured on the job, alongside Pop Duval and Johnny Marshall (played by George Raft). When Pop is killed, they inform his daughter Fay (Dietrich), a club hostess who seems unfazed by the death of her father. Hank falls for the sultry siren, who in turn falls for Johnny, beginning a moody love triangle and a tale which weaves and winds towards its tragic conclusion.

Manpower, clearly cheaper and more economical than the last three pictures Dietrich had made, is a no frills affair, and to its credit is hugely engaging and wonderfully filmed. Walsh, always a Hollywood pro, applies himself with expertise, never wasting a shot and keeping proceedings exciting from the word go. The performances are brilliant too, with both Raft and Robinson suitably competitive, both off screen and on as it turns out.

Reviews were good too, with The New York Times stating, "With such exceptional material, the Warner blacksmiths couldn't help but make good — good, in this sense — meaning the accomplishment of a tough, fast, exciting adventure film." Other publications praised Dietrich directly. Life said "As the clip joint babe, Marlene Dietrich sings a husky song, crosses a pair of nifty legs, bakes a batch of biscuits and, as has become customary in recent successes, gets slapped around."

Dietrich, treating us to a couple of songs by Frederick Hollander and Frank Loesser, is once again the star of the show, delicately positioning herself between the two potential suitors and exuding style and grace throughout. It's another effortlessly entertaining effort, trademark Dietrich glamour in every way. Even though she is merely at the centre of a typically male dichotomy, she ceases to be a play thing for these two high testosterone macho men. In fact, one might say she is even empowered by the way the men fight and act like fools over her. She is a long way from the constricted environment of von Sternberg, but Dietrich is just as powerful and commanding here as she was in Dishonoured and those early classics.

Manpower is rather buried in time today, remembered as a kind of pulpy B picture, and would rarely if ever get singled out for praise among Marlene's finest films and screen creations. Yet she is wonderful with what she's given in the script, a cinematic sensation at her mid career peak.

THE LADY IS WILLING (1942)

Dietrich then made a complete turnaround and portrayed a more feeling, human role in The Lady is Willing, directed and produced by Mitchell Leisen. She plays Elizabeth Madden, a woman who yearns for a child of her own but has no husband. When she finds an abandoned baby, Elizabeth decides to raise it. But as she finds motherhood more difficult than she had imagined, she seeks the aid of paediatrician Corey McBain (played by Fred MacMurray), who just happens to be divorced and clued up about how to raise little ones.

Though given little to do in her previous film Manpower except to provide glamour and seduction (which, I might add, she did more than competently), Dietrich was given the rare chance to flex her acting muscles this time around, to portray a woman who was more sympathetic a character, and show the world she was capable of much more than the stylised sirens, nymphs and femme fatales that had made her famous in the previous decade. She excels in her role wonderfully, adding dimensions to the Dietrich sphere not even suggested in her iconic work of the 1930s. It has to be said she interacts with the now obscure MacMurray brilliantly, and the pair make a likeable duo.

Leisen directs well, but the film is partly let down by a script which is often a little too unimaginative. Penned by James Edward Grant and Albert McCleery, the picture does tend to slacken a little at various points, but Dietrich lifts it from possible depths of mediocrity and ensures it's an enjoyably daft, typical 40s screwball comedy.

The only real paradox here which threatens to ruin the whole thing is the fact that even in this kind of everyday scenario, Dietrich is still adorned in lavish, often ludicrously glamorous costumes, not to mention the interesting choice of head wear. That said, it all adds to the experience of seeing the still exotic and sensational Dietrich trying to get by as a mother. She had, of course, been a sympathetic mother in 1932's Blonde Venus, but in von Sternberg's picture she was also a wild child who went off the rails, only realising after a long journey across the world and into her soul that her family was what she wanted all along. Here, she is more grounded, dedicated to raising the child as best she can. Dietrich pulls it off wonderfully.

Reviews were good, but most attention and praise went on Dietrich herself, who impressed critics with her unlikely but totally believable portrayal. The Brooklyn Daily Eagle wrote "A versatile actress, Marlene Dietrich, a likeable personality and an effective player makes her Liza Madden a credible figure." Others were still more in awe of her looks, such as The New York Daily News, who exclaimed, "She is, if possible, more breathtakingly beautiful than ever, in a sympathetic role that permits her a little wider range of acting than her other vehicles. She moves from light comedy to pathos a little awkwardly, but this is less her fault than the scenarists."

The film may not have been perfect, but Marlene was certainly brilliant in it. The Lady is Willing has fallen by the wayside today, buried in the vaults of time, but fans of Dietrich and the early 40s era of comedy should seek this out and give it a chance.

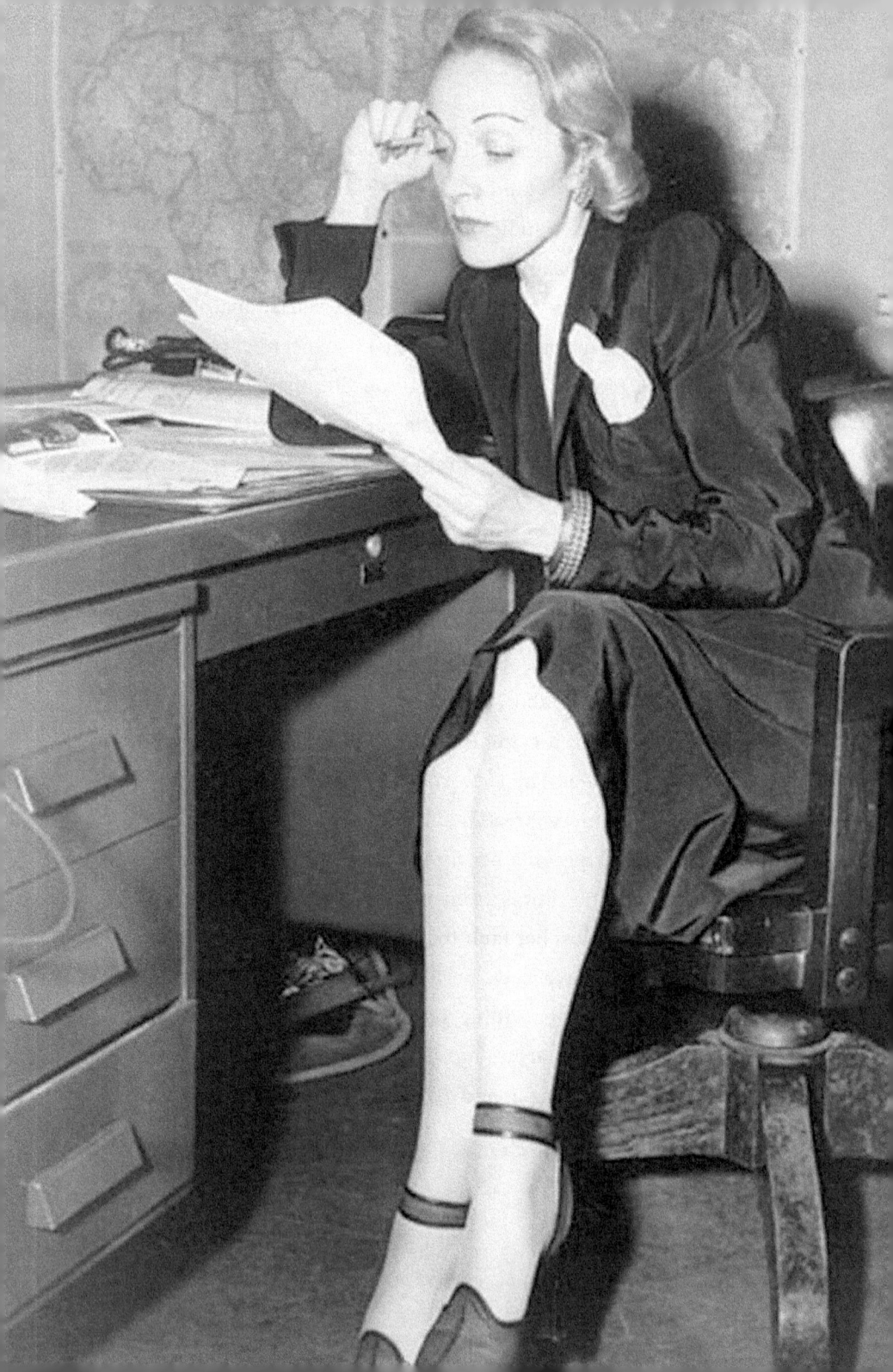

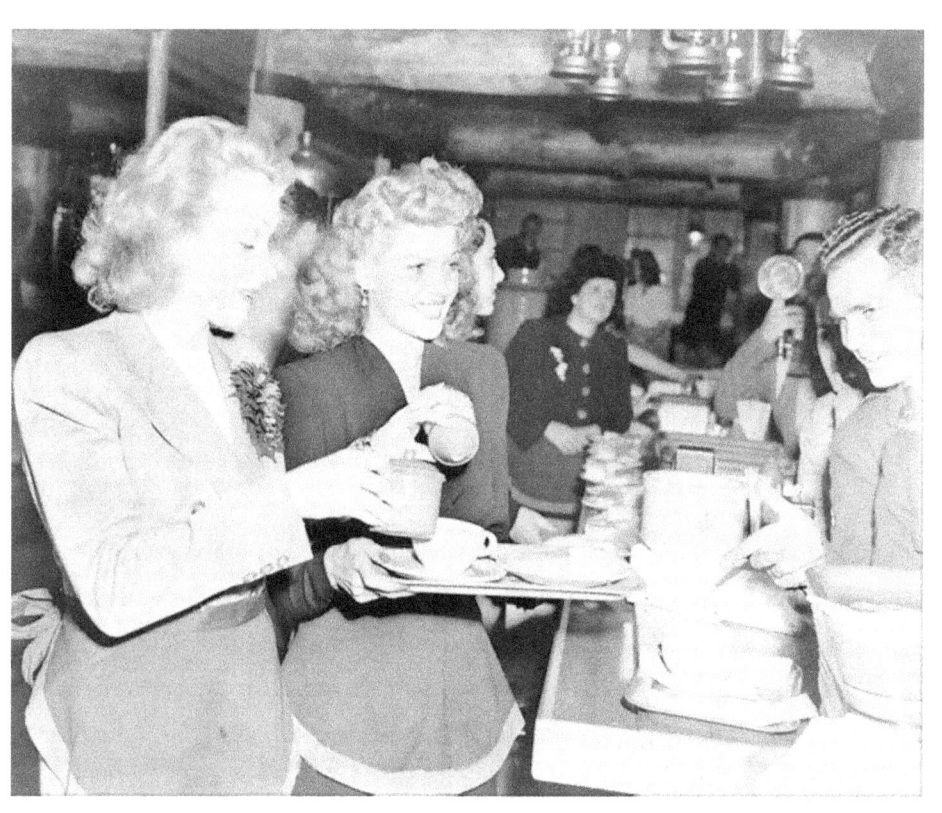

With Rita Hayworth at the Hollywood Canteen

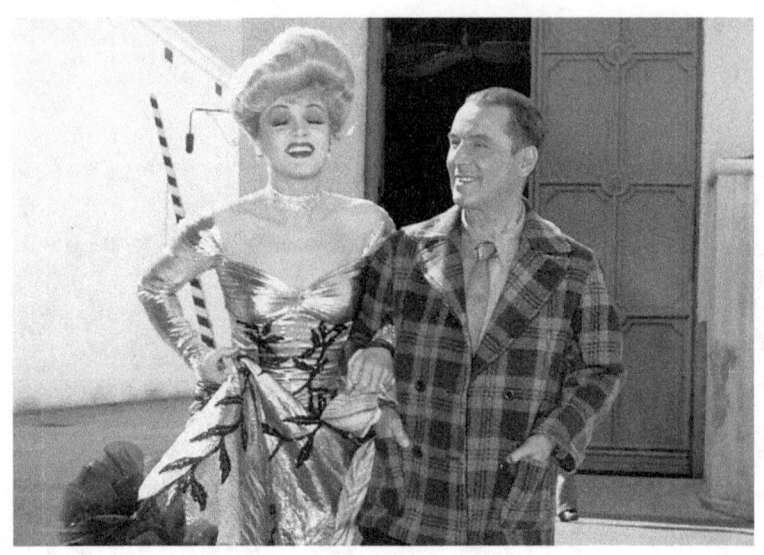

THE SPOILERS (1942)

Dietrich was back with John Wayne again in Ray Enright's The
Spoilers, the second of three films she made with the Duke and the
first of two in quick succession with both Wayne and Randolph Scott.
Adapted from Rex Beach's novel by screenwriter Lawrence Hazard,
this handsomely presented Universal production was the fourth
cinematic telling of the tale (previous versions had been released in
1914, 23 and 30), and it also wasn't to be the last. It is, however, the
best.

The story takes place in Alaska in the year 1900, with Marlene
playing sexy saloon owner Cherry Malotte. Two men arrive in town
saying they have been claim-jumped, so Cherry meets with Alex
McNamara (Scott), the gold commissioner who has a soft spot for
Cherry, who in turn is dedicated to Roy Glennister (John Wayne),
who has just got back from Europe. Sadly, Roy is now more

interested in Judge Stillman's niece Helen (Margaret Lindsay), and Cherry reacts with jealousy at her old beau's new infatuation and throws him out. A plot develops concerning the fight for a gold claim as McNamara reveals his shadier, more corrupt side.

Enright directs with expertise and the whole production looks and feels genuinely great. The sets are tremendous, some of the best of the era in fact, and the art direction earned the film an Oscar nomination. In many ways though, as good as the background is, it is precisely that, background on to which the stars shine. Wayne is as solid as ever, as is Randolph Scott, but again Dietrich is the star. It's impossible to take your eyes off her in this one, with her various fetching outfits and formidable manner. The only mistake here though, for me at least, is the fact they failed to give Dietrich a song, though one can hear a Destry Rides Again number in the mix at one point. It may have seemed an odd idea on paper to put this very German glamour icon, deeply associated with the 1930s, in the setting of another western, but as was proven film after film, Marlene fit the era perfectly somehow, and her exoticism seemed to stick out even more in this sort of backdrop.

At the time it was a nicely sized hit, and Dietrich, while not attracting as many good notices as in her earlier westerns, still earned some praise, even if the New York Times made the rather misguided comment that she was in the tradition of Mae West with her double entendres. They could not have been more wrong of course, for Dietrich was a completely different beast to West and very much her own creation. In conclusion, The Spoilers is a very engaging film, and taken as it is - in its era and genre - it's hard to find a fault.

PITTSBURGH (1942)

By 1942, Marlene Dietrich was already showing her solidarity for the country that had embraced her, made her a star and given her a good life. She denounced her German citizenship at the outbreak of World War 2, turned down a big deal from the German film industry offering a ludicrous sum of money and began getting involved in the war effort, selling war bonds, entertaining troops and spending time with the artillery. Compared to this vital role which she took on with passion, pride and vigour, the movies began to feel inconsequential, an area where she made her money and that was that. In truth, she was already falling out of love with the movies.

That said, she was still making solid pictures. In 1942's Pittsburgh, she was directed by Lewis Seiler and cast once again alongside John Wayne and Randolph Scott, this time in a drama centred on Pittsburgh's steel industry. Wayne plays Charles Markham, a man with aspirations, firstly working as a coal miner but soon climbing the ladder when he realises riches and materialism are more important to him than his friends and loved ones. Again, it offers a moral conclusion - be careful how you treat people on the way up, because you are going to meet them again on the way down. When Charles' riches begin to collapse, he makes a drastic U turn and tries to claw back his relations and credibility. Meanwhile he loses the woman he should have been with, Josie Winters (Dietrich) to his rival, John Evans (Randolph Scott), and begins to see the error of his ways and the fatality of single minded greed. As the war begins, he works for Evans' new company under a different name. Though they clash once again, it is Dietrich who tells them to forget their differences and put the greater good of the country, now fully involved in the war, first in their priorities. The clever twist here is when the trio do make friends again, Wayne's character insists on becoming a partner in Scott's company, perhaps the final and most important comment on his arrogant individualism.

Pittsburgh is definitely, first and foremost, a patriotic film about solidarity, and it is this aspect which obviously attracted Dietrich to the picture. Though like in Manpower she at the centre of a macho power struggle, she gives the film its true depth, a role much more complex than the glamour pusses and sirens of her early Hollywood years. Here she gives a well rounded effort, still very much Dietrich but more believable as a woman from a humble background trying to do the best for the people she cares about.

Unfortunately, though a modest hit, it did not receive good reviews, perhaps because its blatant message often over took the film as entertainment. Though New York Herald Tribune commended Dietrich for her "fetchingly seductive" qualities, Eye For Film wrote at the time, "This is an unashamed propaganda film to inspire workers to work harder in order to help the war effort. The story is predictable and dated and it is hard to ignore the message that is driven home: that the greater good (i.e. the war effort) is more important than individual wealth and petty entanglements."

Today however, nearly 80 years since its release, separated from its era and the mood of the times, Pittsburgh is a decent drama with some essential issues explored in a mature manner. Nicely played, it remains one of the last great Dietrich movies.

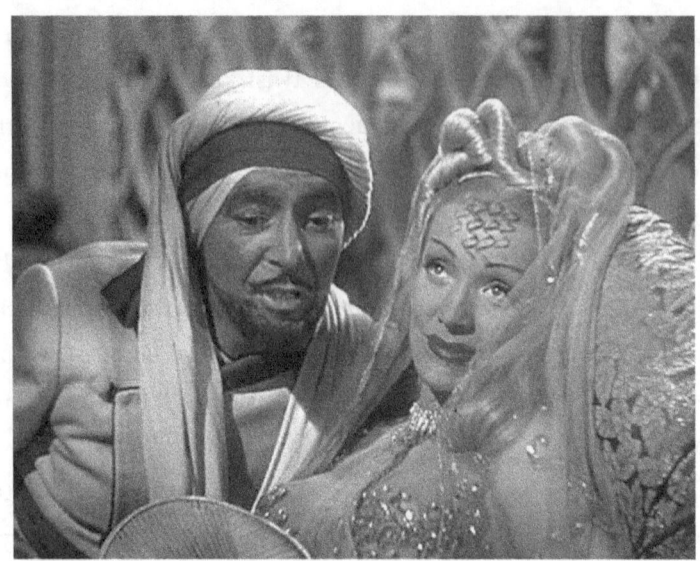

KISMET (1944)

Dietrich was back in glorious colour once again for the visual spectacle Kismet, a film which pulled no punches in its rainbow assortment of shades and refused to tone things down in the slightest. Directed by William Dieterle and written by Edward Noblock and John Meehan (from Knoblock's play) it was the fourth time Kismet had hit the screen. Though some viewers will have been over awed by the Technicolor beauty, it was not a success. For Dietrich however, it was like a mini reunion. She had worked with the director twenty years earlier in the German silent film, Man by the Wayside. Here they were in very different circumstances, and it could be said the pair deserved a better movie.

Ronald Colman plays Hafiz, a beggar magician in Baghdad who wants to make his daughter a princess. Marsinah (Joy Ann Page) is having a liaison with the son of a gardener (James Craig), who actually turns out to be the Caliph of Baghdad incognito. Dietrich plays the queen of the castle of the Grand Vizier, and has been having an affair with Hafiz who in turn has been pretending to be the Prince of Hassir. This farcical web of deceit makes way for a rich and over the top drama that in no way can be taken remotely seriously. As daft as it is however, it keeps you invested until the end. The main reasons to watch it though are for the colour, the garish, unashamedly bright sets and costumes, and of course for Dietrich herself who, surrounded by solid talents, rises above everyone and illuminates as a true star. It is not one of her most complex characterisations, not by any means, but it is high camp at its best, and her costumes have to be seen to be believed.

Perhaps the highlight comes when Dietrich, her famous legs painted gold, performs a wild dance that briefly elevates the picture to another level. This scene gave Dietrich one of her minor legendary moments, but it's buried in a film which isn't really worthy of it. The film gained some pleasant notices and Dietrich herself attracted praise, though most reviews reminded us of the good work Marlene was doing for the troops, a job she evidently took much more seriously than all this motion picture nonsense. The New York Times bluntly commented that it was worth watching mainly for Dietrich's legs, while Variety said that Colman outshone Dietrich and made her nothing more than a stooge.

Whichever way you look at it, this is nothing but shallow escapism and it would be foolish to try to look for anything deeper than pure silliness.

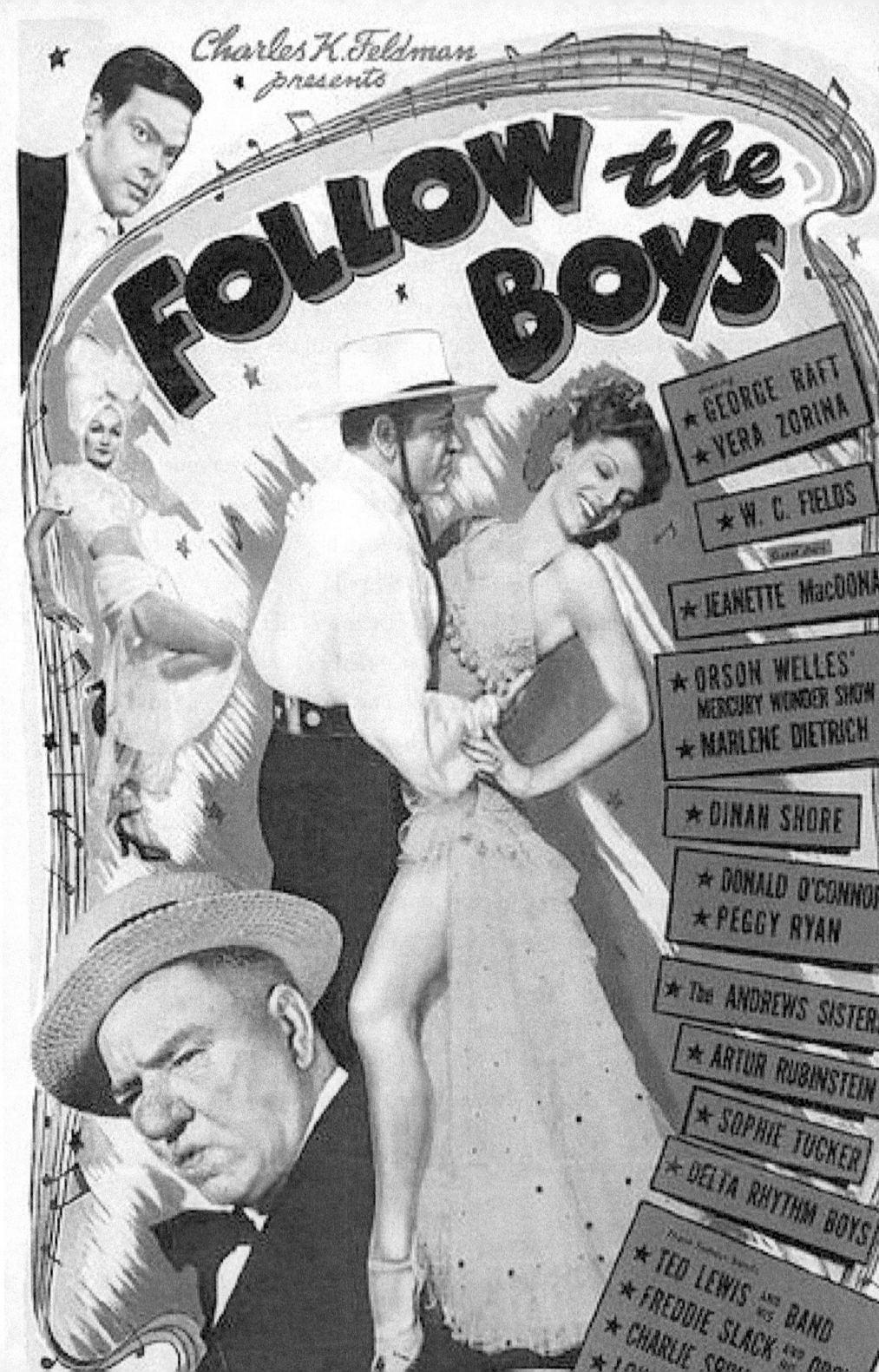

FOLLOW THE BOYS (1944)

The same year she starred in the lavish and wonderfully over the top Kismet, Dietrich appeared in Follow the Boys. The film was made to boost morale of American troops who were fighting the good fight, and almost everyone who was anyone at the time signed up for the effort. Also known as Three Cheers for the Boys, it is an unashamedly patriotic picture, though it thankfully harbours no hidden agenda or propaganda message.

The project began in June of 1943, when producer Charles K Feldman began to put it together and won the services of George Raft, who would be playing vaudeville performer Tony West who makes his way to Hollywood after seeing first hand the decline of music hall. The plot, if one can call it that, makes way for a series of cameos and set pieces, each one as memorable as the last. The various stars include WC Fields, Sophie Tucker and Donald O Connor.

Though I may be a little biased, the highlight for me is certainly the magic act scene featuring Orson Welles and Dietrich herself. Dietrich here joins Welles' famous Mercury Wonder Show (a magic act he entertained the troops with, sometimes featuring Marlene and other times his current wife, Rita Hayworth) and takes part in a wonderful sequence where she is sawn in half. Orson and Marlene were great friends in real life and they would work together again, much more memorably in fact, in 1958's Touch of Evil (directed by Welles). That said, their scene together in Follow the Boys is simply wonderful and it would take a downbeat soul not to be raised by it.

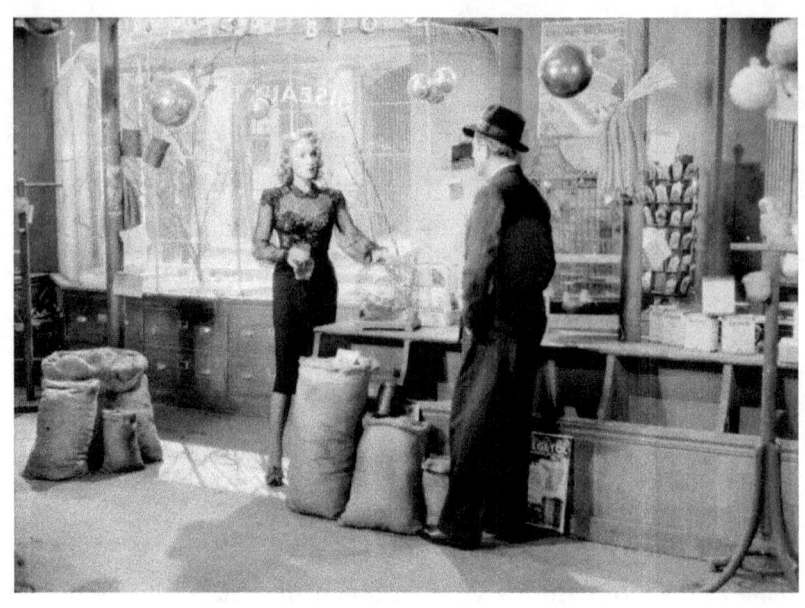

MARTIN ROUMAGNAC (1946)

The war now over, and her fine work during the conflict cemented in the annals of history, Dietrich decided to take a starring role opposite the great French actor Jean Gabin, with whom she was having a relationship, in Martin Roumagnac. Directed by Georges Lacombe, it cast Marlene as Blanche Ferrand, who is due to marry Martin (Gabin), a construction engineer. The pair enjoy a romance until he learns that she lives a double life as a prostitute. Enraged, he kills her, though he is racked by guilt during the trial when he learns she really did genuinely love him. The film ends with a morally troubling climax, when Martin gets off for the crime but winds up getting murdered himself by one of Blanche's old suitors.

Dietrich had been in France at the end of the war and decided to stay there, being cosy with Gabin, signing up for the film with one of the country's leading film icons. There was a lot of hope hanging on the picture, but it was met with harsh reviews and censorship. Clearly, the way the filmmakers openly dealt with prostitution rubbed them up the wrong way. It has the reputation of being something of a disaster and is regularly cited as being Gabin's lowest point. That said, all these years on, if one did not know of the picture's awful reputation, it really isn't so bad. Dietrich is good in her part and while Gabin had been much better in other movies, it isn't the dire mess it's often mythologized to be.

Dietrich herself put the film's failure down to the fact that audiences could not imagine her as such a character, and Marlene's own daughter, Maria Riva, wrote in her marvellous biography of her mother that she is not a believable adventurous. But it was probably more complex than that. Did the world, after getting through such horrors in the Second World War, really want to see such a grim picture, and one featuring Dietrich, a woman who stood for the fun, light and gay thirties before the war, in such glum circumstances? Possibly not. But the film remains important in Dietrich's career, for it marks a turning point; this is Dietrich after the war, after the world divide, after she had seen things she never thought she would see. The Marlene of the glamorous but innocent thirties was gone, and now, vastly approaching fifty (though she still looked great and nowhere near that age), it was time for Dietrich to move into different kinds of roles and make way for younger leading ladies.

Nowhere near Dietrich's finest work, but hardly the stinker it's made out to be.

Anno I - N. 1   *4 agosto 1946*

Confidenze di Liala

LIRE 12 IN TUTTA ITALIA

Settimanale di Novelle, Romanzi e Varietà

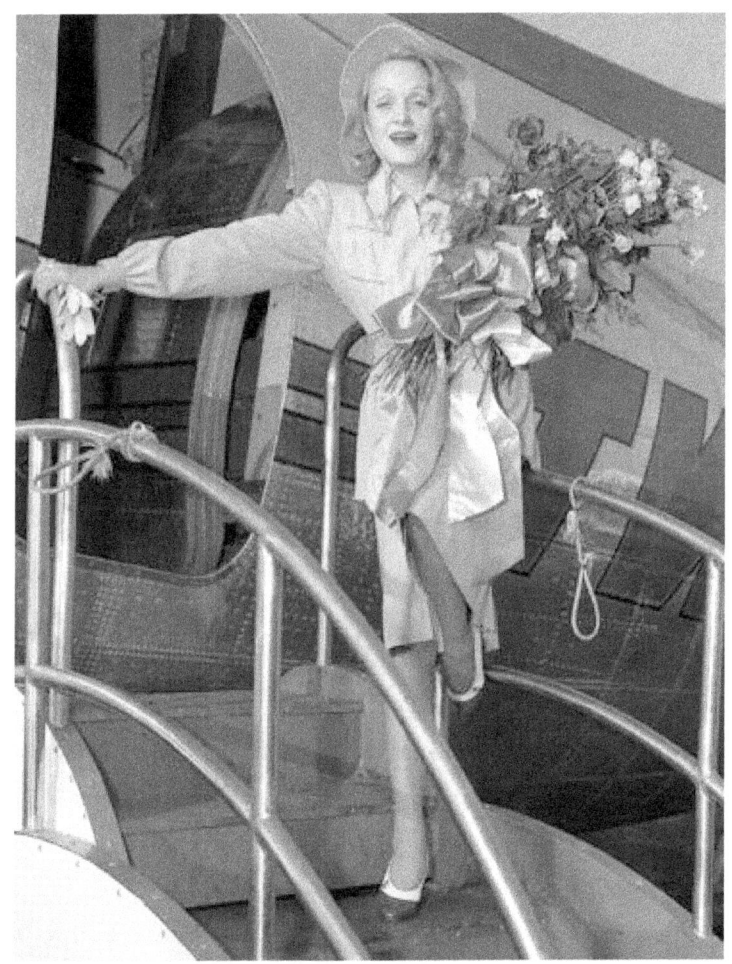

Dietrich in 1946

GOLDEN EARRINGS (1947)

Having not appeared in a Hollywood production since 1944 (three whole years!), Dietrich signed up for Mitchell Leisen's 1947 spy drama, Golden Earrings. Clad in the kind of exotic costumes she might have worn when under the guidance of Josef von Sternberg, Dietrich donned a black wig and gave the part her all. It resulted in her most convincing and effective performance in years.

The film starts in post-war London, with Major Ralph Denistoun (Ray Milland) receiving a package containing some golden earrings. Getting straight on a plane to Paris with a war correspondent, Ralph begins to tell the tale, which begins in pre-war England, involving him and a friend working for British Intelligence going under cover with the Nazis. When they escape in Nazi uniforms, the duo separate and plan to meet up in the Black Forest. As Ralph hides his uniform, he hears the singing of a gypsy. This is where he - and indeed we - gets his first glimpse of Dietrich as Lydia the gypsy, singing a song while mixing a pot. She knows the back roads intimately, and in hooking up with her Ralph sees the perfect opportunity to evade the Nazis to get to his comrade. Lydia, giving him a disguise of his own, begins to lead the way, though he must also now face the gypsy brood of which Lydia is a member.

Lydia remains one of Dietrich's most memorable and well rounded roles. It is a broad part, but Marlene knows what she's doing and manages to measure her performance in keeping with the ridiculous but admittedly engaging surroundings. She is back at her best here, clearly comfortable in these lavish, exaggerated scenarios and getting so comfortably into the role that we believe she is the gypsy one hundred percent. Gone is the cold ice queen of the early thirties, the unfeeling goddess of Shanghai Express; Dietrich is Lydia, the passionate gypsy who has taken it upon herself to get this man to safety. Though Ray Milland received top billing (at that point, believe it or not, he was a bigger name than Dietrich) it was Dietrich who took the spotlight and attracted most of the favourable notices.

As well as being a huge commercial hit in its day, reviews were also positive. Dietrich, though absent from a leading Hollywood role for three years, was as impressive as ever. However, some were still more concerned with her looks and very being than her acting ability. The New York Times wrote, "The fabulous legs of Marlene Dietrich and that lady's distinguished charms, which have not been seen in movies since Kismet, are still rather miserably hidden beneath some bear-grease and a lot of gypsy rags..." The writer, Bosley Crowther, wonders why the studio would go to such lengths to conceal Dietrich's famous physical assets, though he does fail to mention her acting in the film is commendable, so fixed he is on the frustrating costumes.

Golden Earrings is plain fun, an irresistible romp that feels like a breath of fresh air in Dietrich's filmography. She may have started to fall out of love with the movies, but the filmgoers were still very much in love with her, as was the camera itself.

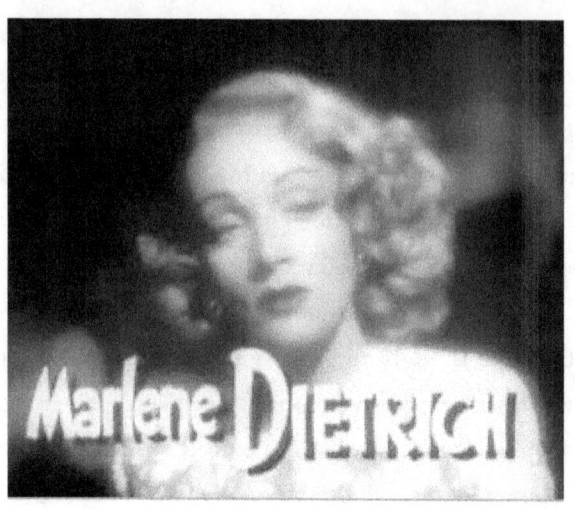

A FOREIGN AFFAIR (1948)

After the high camp glory of Golden Earrings, Dietrich went on to make what many consider to be one of her finest, most accomplished films. Directed by the great Billy Wilder, A Foreign Affair is a classy, graceful romantic comedy. The plot follows John Lund as a US army captain in Berlin who on the one hand pines for former Nazi cafe singer Erika (Marlene Dietrich of course) and a US congresswoman (Jean Arthur).

Wilder, who had served in the army during World War 2, was promised government assistance if he made a film about Germany under the allies. With producer Charles Brackett, he began to put together the idea for A Foreign Affair. For Wilder, there was only one woman for the role of Erika, and that was Dietrich. A Foreign Affair may have been marketed and presented as a comedy, but it was also a rather serious film, essentially for the position in which it placed Marlene herself. Dietrich, who had so publicly damned the Nazis and what they had done during the war, was a perfect choice for the part of Erika, but it was a brave move on Wilder's part to even think of approaching the pro-US star. Wilder recalled visiting Dietrich and offering her the role, insisting she was the woman for the job. "She kept making criticisms and suggestions... and finally I said, like I had thought of it just that moment, 'Marlene, only *you* can play this part.' And she agreed with me..."

During filming it's been reported that Jean Arthur was jealous of the supposedly preferential treatment Wilder was giving Dietrich. She got so annoyed that she even refused to watch the film, though it was a decision she later reversed, calling Wilder after eventually seeing it and complimenting him on his work. But Wilder really did love Dietrich, and in many interviews spoke fondly of her as one of the greatest people he had ever worked with. "The crews adored her," he recalled. "She liked to find somebody with a cold, so she could make chicken soup for him. She loved to cook."

The film was another hit, making this something of a commercially fruitful era for Dietrich. Reviews were glowing, with Life calling it a "triumphant return" for Marlene, adding that there were definite links to The Blue Angel and her role as Lola Lola. Any similarities though, were coincidental. Of course Wilder was aware of her myth and her importance in film history. But Lola Lola was a million miles away from the former Nazi Eika. Even if Wilder intended her role as partly a homage to her rich past (let's not forget, The Blue Angel was almost twenty years old at this point), her place in A Foreign Affair is far from novel. This is one of her finest pieces of acting, in a film which deserves to last and not be buried in time.

JIGSAW (1949)

Marlene Dietrich then took another cameo appearance in Fletcher Markle's low budget independent film, Jigsaw. Financed by the producers and the film's star, Franchot Tone, it featured him as a District Attorney who uncovers a hate group while investigating a murder. Dietrich's appearance comes when Tone's character goes to a club called Blue Angel, and she happens to briefly walk past their table, while Henry Fonda, in another blink and you'll miss him cameo, plays the waiter Dietrich passes.

The film is really only worth seeing for these star appearances and is hopelessly dated today. It remains something of an oddity, coming across as a vanity project for Tone. It is also buried in time and is very obscure indeed, though a pirated DVD of it can be purchased online if one wants to complete their Dietrich collection.

Bosley Crowther of the New York Times wrote of the film: "On the sole account of Jigsaw, which opened at the Mayfair on Saturday, Hollywood has no reason to look immediately and anxiously to its laurels... It is sluggishly directed by Fletcher Markle, who also co-authored the script, and almost indifferently played, where good playing would do the most for it, by Franchot Tone in the principal role... An irresistible temptation to get a few recognizable stars to play bit roles in the picture was accepted unfortunately."

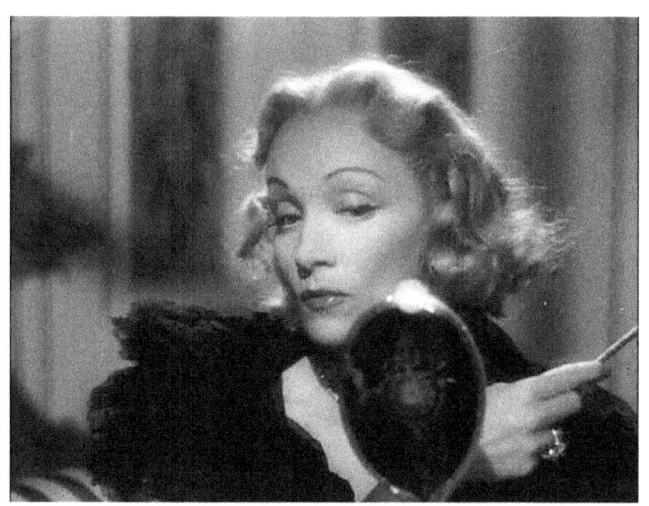

STAGE FRIGHT (1950)

One thing people may overlook about Dietrich is the fact that she worked for/with some of the greatest directors of various Hollywood periods. Consider her early iconic work for von Sternberg for instance, her two roles for Billy Wilder (A Foreign Affair and the later Witness for the Prosecution), her appearance in Touch of Evil for Orson Welles and in Rancho Notorious for the legendary Fritz Lang. Few of these names however, especially retrospectively, measure up to the mighty influence and importance of the man who directed her in 1950's Stage Fright, the iconic genius Alfred Hitchcock.

Stage Fright is rarely talked about in Hitchcock's oeuvre today, it being released in a somewhat awkward period for the master of suspense. Alfred had been working in Hollywood since 1939 after coming over from England, where he had made some of his best work in my view. He had recently formed his own Production

Company, Transatlantic Pictures, and directed Rope (1948) and Under Capricorn (1949), neither of which was very successful. He followed these mixed experiments with Stage Fright, a film which saw him returning to his London roots, it being filmed in various locations across the English capital. It was also a more straight forward thriller, with comic overtones, directed in the trademark Hitch style.

The plot concerns Richard Todd as a man who is accused of murdering the husband of the woman he has fallen in love with, the exotic music star Charlotte Inwood, played by a charismatic and commanding Marlene Dietrich. Jane Wyman plays Eve, a friend who agrees to help clear his name and prove he really wasn't the killer. The plot thickens and though the situation looks more and more hopeless for our accused man, things begin to unravel and the truth is revealed.

Though Stage Fright is often completely overlooked when people discuss essential Hitchcock, it is a solid thriller and is among his most enjoyably eccentric works. The plot twists and turns, there are genuine surprises delivered in the trademark Hitchcock way, but there is also a lot of humour too, much of it mischievous. An added bonus is the presence of Alistair Sim as Eve's father, a dotty old soul who lives by the sea and inserts some old fashioned English charm into proceedings. The two leads are fabulous, but again, the whole thing is dominated by Dietrich. At this point it may have become something of a cliché to state Dietrich steals the show, but in Stage Fright, even when she is not on screen, the very idea of her looms large and we are waiting for her next appearance. As the star singer, she is playing a variation on herself, a diva in the truest sense who

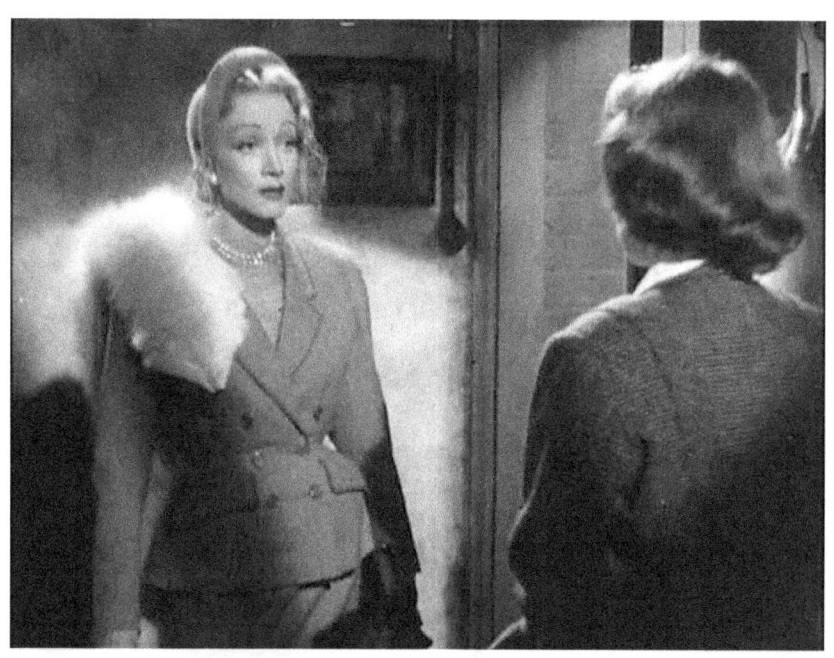

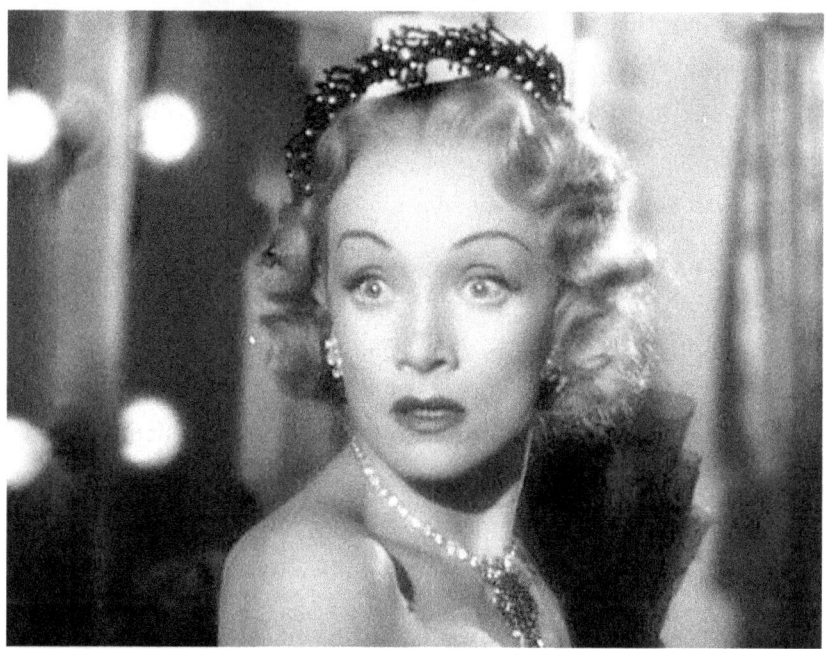

demands - sometimes without having to say anything - star treatment. And she got it with Mr. Hitchcock, who was aware of the power of Dietrich and was willing to do anything to make sure she was not only on board but totally comfortable during production. She may have played the awkward demanding star at times, but ultimately Hitchcock got brilliant results from her. She was, in his view, worth all the fuss. "Miss Dietrich has that spark that transmits itself visually," he later said. "It's rare."

The film was a commercial success, especially in the UK, where Dietrich was still a hugely popular figure, as was Hitch himself. Reviews at the time singled Dietrich out too. New York Herald Tribune were impressed, stating "It is Miss Dietrich, though, who dominates Stage Fright. She sings sultry songs and charms all her gentlemen callers throughout the work." They did add however, "It is only a pity that she and Hitchcock could not have found a more substantial frame..."

Perhaps, if things had been different, Dietrich could easily have been in one of Hitchcock's Stateside thrillers, filling the role of the female in any number of his more important and acclaimed pictures. That said, as her personality was so large, it's hard to imagine her as James Stewarts' belle in Rear Window or similar roles. Here, within the confines of the thriller, Hitchcock managed to use Marlene in a way that her larger than life personality was included in the film, and didn't feel too big or out of place, where reality and fiction blurred. She was Charlotte Inwood, but she was also Marlene Dietrich. It's a masterful bit of performance, and her rendition of Cole Porter's The Laziest Gal in Town is worth the price of admission alone.

It is worth noting that Dietrich demanded - and indeed got - choice of camera angles and shots. One can sense the hand of Dietrich at play, for she is always photographed from the best angles and put in the finest light. Still, her appearances are effective throughout the picture, and rather than being unnecessary star brattishness, the lighting works in favour of the harsh character, equally glamorous and untrustworthy. Hitchcock himself said of the set-up, "Everything is fine. Miss Dietrich has arranged the whole thing. She has told them exactly where to place the lights and how to photograph her." Later on he added of her, "Marlene was a professional star. She was also a professional cameraman, art director, editor, costume designer, hairdresser, makeup woman, composer, producer and director."

It was later reported that Dietrich found Hitchcock a slightly odd fellow. Whether it's true or not, they worked well in their sole collaboration and it is a pity they didn't go on to do more films together.

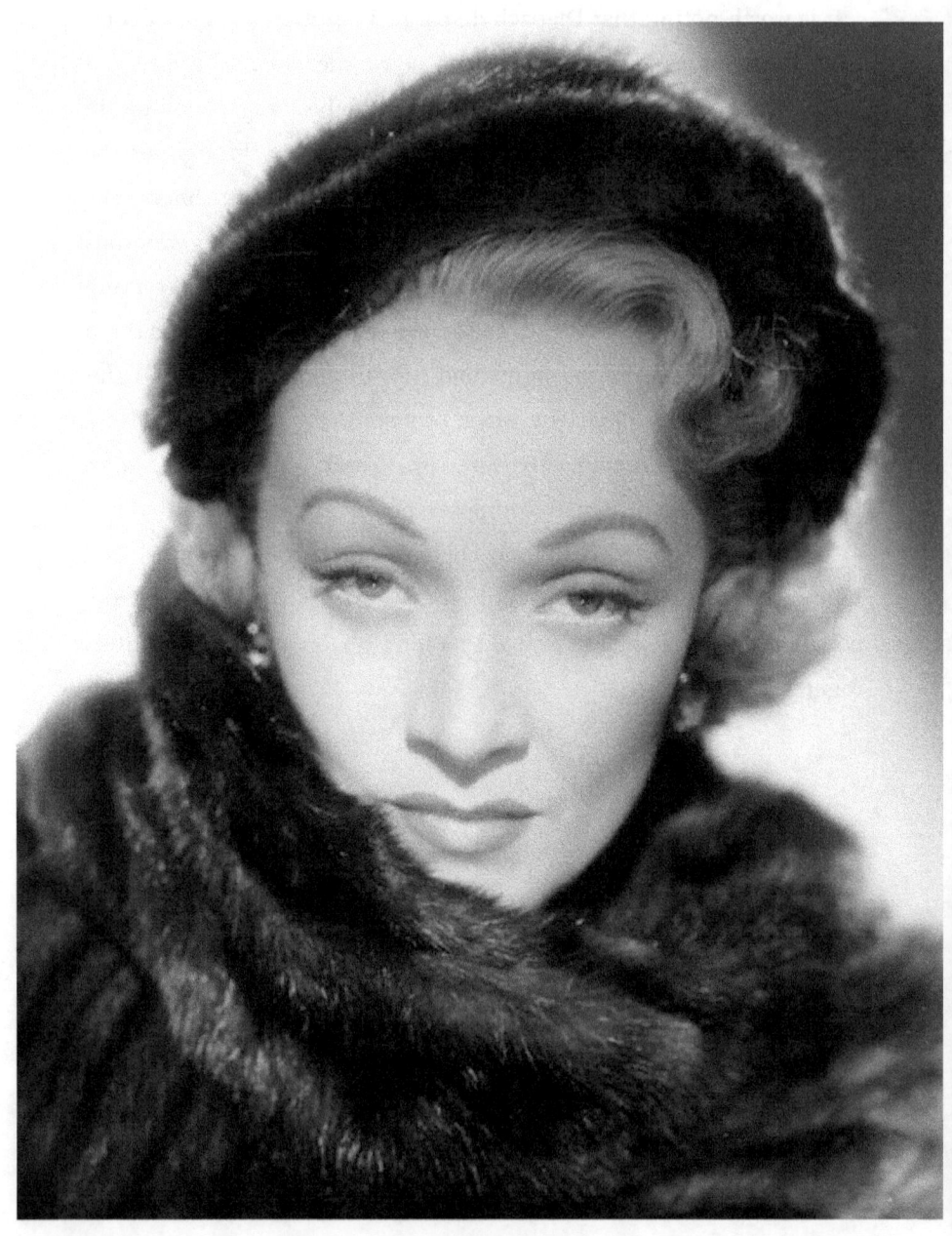

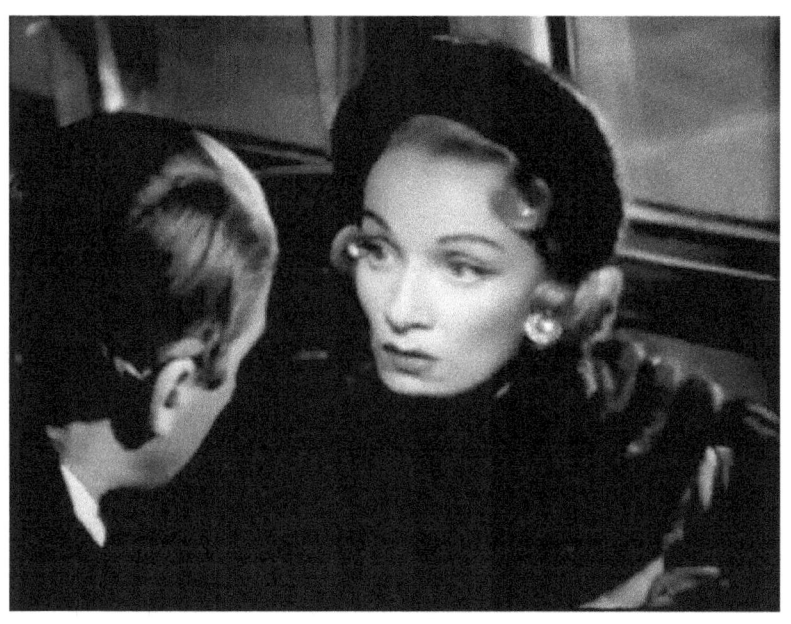

NO HIGHWAY IN THE SKY (1951)

Few actresses were still making good work, if not some of their best, into their fifties, but Marlene Dietrich was certainly getting through some solid movies as the decades went on. Straight after working with the great Hitchcock, she was back with her old Destry Rides Again pal James Stewart on Henry Koster's hugely enjoyable No Highway in the Sky, known simply as No Highway in the States.

Based on the novel by Nevil Shute, it stars James Stewart as Royal Aircraft specialist Theodore Honey, who is sent to examine why a plane crashed in Labrador, Canada. Citing the problem as an issue with metal fatigue, tests are performed which determine the strain a plane endures after an eight hour flight. Later, when Theodore is on a flight himself, he realises the journey is nearing the time it takes for metal fatigue to kick in. Becoming increasingly terrified that his theory might be true, he alerts everyone on board to the situation, including the glamorous Hollywood actress, Monica Teasdale, played brilliantly by Dietrich. Will Theodore's theory be proven correct, or will his eccentric behaviour land him in deep trouble?

Producer Buddy Lighton commissioned Oscar Millard to pen the screenplay, and he took six months to perfect it. Robert Donat was originally lined up to play Theodore, but at short notice Stewart replaced him. Stewart provided the manic, often bumbling energy, while Marlene put forth the style and seductive glamour. In exotic costumes and again, like in Stage Fright, always presented as a star to be in awe of, she fills the role perfectly, playing another variant on herself, though definitely a supporting part to Stewart's more showy, often over the top and occasionally comedic performance.

Biographies on Dietrich have documented diva-ish behaviour, and a certain discomfort with British co star Glynis Johns, but as this book focuses primarily on the films and her performances, it's best to keep the behind the scenes gossip to one side. This is one of Dietrich's last great roles, a confident and assured effort in a decade where she was gliding from one to gem to another, at least for a short while.

The film was yet another box office success. Clearly, Dietrich was on a roll. Reviews were good too, and once again Marlene got singled out for her work. Some reviewers were happy to see her providing "throaty glamour", while Variety noted that "Miss Dietrich, as a noted film actress, stands out in a very sympathetic role."

This was a big contrast compared to her harsh, cold and calculating Charlotte in Hitchcock's Stage Fright, and here she is right beside the hero, sharing his worries throughout. Anyone under the impression that Dietrich was a one trick pony, a cool if not cold Teutonic figure who was distanced from the viewer in both her beauty and the way she was presented to us as some kind of living work of art, need only line up her best work to see the variety in her roles; think of the bawdy liveliness of her Frenchy in Destry Rides Again, the heartless Charlotte in Stage Fright, the former Nazi in A Foreign Affair and here, as the famous but approachable film star, and one will see a vast range of types, all of which she excels in. In No Highway in the Sky, she provides the stable, grounded quality to Stewart's often wild and untamed efforts.

As a film, No Highway in the Sky is one of the finest pictures Dietrich ever appeared in, a solid and gripping drama that flows nicely and provides laughs, thrills and spills all the way to its conclusion. Her second and final pairing with Stewart, it's a minor moment of movie magic, well worth revisiting.

RANCHO NOTORIOUS (1952)

Rancho Notorious saw Marlene Dietrich returning to the western genre, this time with German legend Fritz Lang in the director's chair. Originally named The Legend of Chuck-a-Luck, Howard Hughes, then the head of RKO Pictures, insisted on the name Rancho Notorious, perhaps wisely in retrospect.

The film certainly looks wonderful, its Technicolor splendour still dazzling to this day, but there is something slightly tired, predictable and underwhelming about the film itself. Arthur Kennedy is Vern, a rancher who goes on the hunt for his fiancée's killer. He winds up in Rancho Notorious, a sanctuary for outlaws, run by the formidable Alder Keane, played by a scene stealing Marlene Dietrich.

As flawed as the film is, Dietrich is faultless in her portrayal of the philosophical woman of mystery, a role which is almost a pre-echo of the wise and reflective gypsy fortune telling madam from Touch of Evil. She is so good in the film here that everyone else kind of shrinks away, and whenever she is in a scene all attention remains on her. Even into the 1950s, with Dietrich's von Sternberg era twenty years behind her, she was as powerful as ever, a true screen presence.

Most reviews were very critical. The New York Times were not impressed, writing, "In the department of western action, the show has its interesting points, including a couple of fist-and-gun fights that have been racily staged by Fritz Lang. Anyone who will settle for stick-ups and slug fests and pistol duels, all in Technicolor, may find enough in this picture to satiate his lust. Hungry-looking actors swagger and snarl in the outlaw roles. But anyone who expects a western picture to match the character of its able female star had better look in another direction. This one is run-of-the-mill."

Variety were underwhelmed too, seeing it as a pale imitation of Destry Rides Again. "This Marlene Dietrich western has some of the flavour of the old outdoor classics without fully capturing their quality and magic. The characters play the corny plot straight." Even they however had to admit that Marlene was still effective, even if the film itself was lacking. "Dietrich is as sultry and alluring as ever," they wrote. "Dietrich is a dazzling recreation of the old time saloon mistress, and handles her song, Get Away, Young Man, with her usual throaty skill."

Dietrich had been friends with Fritz Lang for years and it was about time they got to work together. Though Lang made better films, and the western was hardly the ideal setting for him, the man does well with what he is given and also gets the best out of his dynamic star. Dietrich certainly has her moments in this one, a sadder and more wistful Frenchy in some ways, but the movie itself was undeserving of such a strong effort. Not her best work then, but proof that she was still a force to be reckoned with.

AROUND THE WORLD IN 80 DAYS (1956)

Then film work began to phase out. Marlene Dietrich had already begun to slow down her movie commitments and develop her new career as a cabaret artist in the early fifties, a job she pursued with typical gusto and passion until the mid 1970s when ill health and injuries forced her to retire. Bored with film, Dietrich, perhaps aware that the good roles would not be coming way her now she was approaching sixty, adapted surprisingly well to her new life as The Dietrich, the larger than life performer who toured the world, becoming the highest paid cabaret act of all time.

But film appearances still came, though much less often now. In 1956 she appeared in the star studded adventure epic, Around the World in 80 Days, directed by Michael Anderson and starring David Niven as Phileas Fogg. It was a huge success and won Best Picture at the Oscars. It was by far the most successful film Dietrich had been involved with in her whole career, though her part was all too brief it has to be said. Playing a variation on her dance hall image, Dietrich shines as best she can, illuminating the film with her star quality for the small segment she is on screen. There were so many stars however - from Buster Keaton to Frank Sinatra - that it was impossible for Dietrich to make too big an impression. Still, it was a fun role and a nice diversion for Marlene (and nice pay check as well), who was already becoming one of the globe's most popular stage acts.

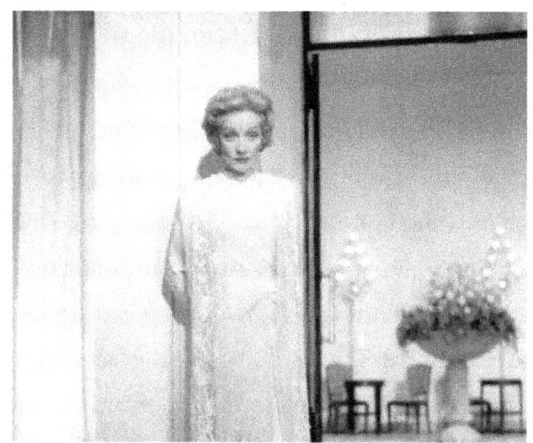

THE MONTE CARLO STORY (1956)

She had made her only French film with Jean Gabin in 1946, and here, eleven years on, she starred in her sole Italian production, alongside the hugely popular director-actor Vittorio De Sica. Among her most obscure works, it's also one of her least acclaimed movies, and some might even call it undistinguished. Director Samuel Taylor tries his best with a tired plot, but the film falls short of being that memorable, despite the potential brilliance of the two stars.

In the French Riviera, Dietrich is the aspirational gal with no money who comes across Count Fiabe (De Sica), riddled with gambling debts but insistent that this beautiful woman is the meal ticket he has been looking for.

It's hard to get too enthusiastic about this one, a film which tries hard but cannot hold the star power of Dietrich, who deserves so much more than this lacklustre production. If this is what she was being offered, there is little wonder she was mostly sticking to the stage work.

WITNESS FOR THE PROSECUTION (1957)

Dietrich was back with the great Billy Wilder for her next film, 1957's Witness for the Prosecution, a solid film which also the last truly great starring role she had in a picture. Based on the play by Agatha Christie, this court room set drama was ahead of its time and went on to influence dozens of movies. The great Charles Laughton plays barrister Wilfried Robarts, who takes on the case of Leonard Vole (Tyrone Power), who has been accused of murdering a rich widow named Emily French. Dietrich plays Leonard's wife, Christine, a distant and self contained woman who comes forth with a rather thin alibi for her husband. At the end of the trial however, it comes as a great shock when she is called up as a witness.

Powerfully adapted by Wilder and two screenwriters Larry Marcus and Harry Kurnitz, Witness for the Prosecution is a film to see for the dialogue, the contained, measured pace and the brilliant - dare I say unmatched in this kind of setting - performances, particularly from the mesmerising and effortlessly engaging Charles Laughton. His is a master-class in film acting, holding every bit of your attention with every syllable he utters.

Dietrich is wonderful too, threatening to steal the whole picture with a dazzling display of versatility. Maybe it's because she was acting alongside a true powerhouse on the scale of Laughton, and she had no choice but to up her game, but it's arguable that this is perhaps Dietrich's finest ever performance. Not stylised in any way, nor lazily applied with breezy starriness, Dietrich gets right under the skin of her character and makes her multifaceted and entirely believable. This is a tour de force in every way, and maybe the most accomplished one she ever put to film. She received a Golden Globe nomination for work, and it has to be said, she should have walked home with the gong.

In other ways, it's a totally Dietrich-esque performance. She's often clad in eye catching attire, in particular the long black dress with the slit that shows off those famously glorious legs, and we are even treated to a Marlene song in the form of I May Never Go Home Anymore. The scene where she is disguised as the cockney woman is also illustrative of her surprising range.

The movie was a critical hit, a box office success and also popular with the award organisations. Dietrich's work was well received all around, with Films in Review setting the tone of the notices with the statement, "Marlene Dietrich proves that she is a dramatic actress as well as a still glamorous chanteuse." The New York Herald Tribune, long time appreciators of Dietrich's films, wrote she was "a sultry siren. She plays it with fire and finesse."

Today, the film is still hugely popular, often making lists of great movies of the era and Top 5's of the courtroom genre. During a DVD re-release in 2007, The Times wrote that "Marlene Dietrich was never better than she is here", and they definitely had a point. This wasn't the last great Dietrich role as such (more were to come, of course), but it was her last great major acting part, and if it was a goodbye to an era - when Dietrich held a picture and kept the audience in the palm of her hand - then it was a perfect swan song.

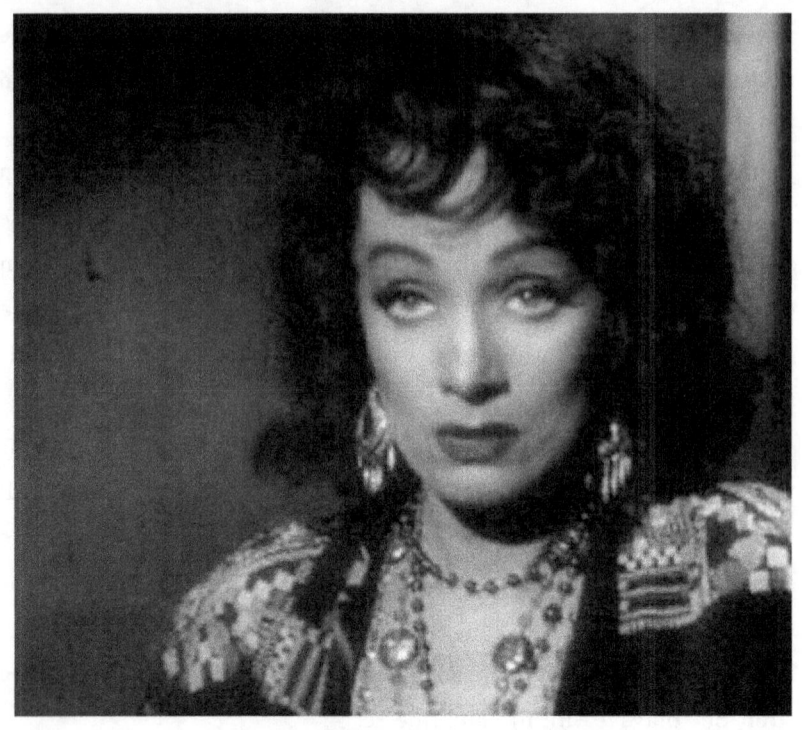

TOUCH OF EVIL (1958)

"It's the eighth one!" Welles said at the time of the release of Touch of
Evil, speaking of directing in general and keeping his integrity intact.
In the interview he diminishes all aspects of a movie in favour of the
importance of the edit. "You know I've been working for seventeen
years; I have directed eight films and I have edited only three of
them. There are in this film (Touch of Evil) some scenes that I
neither wrote nor directed, of which I know absolutely nothing. Or
my style, for my vision of cinema, the editing is not one aspect, *it is
the aspect.* Directing is an invention of people like you; it is not an art,
or at most an art for a minute a day. This minute is terribly crucial,

but it happens only very rarely. The only moment where one can exercise any control over a film is in the editing. But in the editing room, I work very slowly, which always unleashes the temper of the producers who snatch the film from my hands. I don't know why it takes me so much time: I could work forever on the editing of a film."

Ever since Citizen Kane re wrote the rule book Welles had had to endure the size of his legend and people's disappointments with whatever he had come out with in its wake. The next film Welles found himself directing after several low budget, largely self financed pictures turned out to be Touch of Evil for a major studio, a classic noir tale featuring the man himself in a very showy, larger than life role. By far one of the most important, key works of Welles' career, it follows a winding tale of murder on the border of Mexico. Though Charlton Heston is the lead actor (he plays a drug enforcement official), Welles walks away with the picture in a truly blitzing part as police captain Hank Quinlan. He gets all the best scenes, and the most memorable dialogue, by far the most exciting member of the cast.

As had occurred before, Welles was originally just to be a member of the cast, but Heston claims to have put him forward as the best man for the directing job. According to other sources, in fact according to Welles himself, Orson apparently asked producer Albert Zugsmith for the worst script he had, as if to prove a point that he could make a fine film from a bad screenplay. A part of me wants to believe the latter tale, as it fits so well into Welles folk lore. To be honest though, it's probably Heston's more straight forward memory which is the truth.

During the shoot, Welles proved to be the very embodiment of the free and open "actor's director". Though he claimed it to be an overrated job, he also took great pride in his role as director, and established this story as a respectable piece of cinema, not some seedy B picture sleaze fest. Orson went all out to ensure there was never a dull moment in Touch of Evil.

Vitally, Orson even managed to persuade Marlene Dietrich to help him out and fill the role of the gypsy madam. Originally working for a miniscule amount as a favour to Welles, she insisted on being unbilled. When the studio realised she was on board however, they were adamant she get billing to bring in the punters. Marlene did her work quickly, going from studio to studio to gather wigs and props form her previous films to flesh out the enigmatic role. In truth she has some of the best scenes in the film, dazzlingly beautiful in her black wig. Her main scene with Welles, when he comes in drunk asking for her to read his fortune is pure gold; as is her final scene, when she boldly says of the deceased Welles, "He was some kind of man. What does it matter what you say about people?"

Welles later said that he had never fancied Dietrich as a blonde, and the one time he found her attractive was as a brunette in Golden Earrings. Here, he re-creates the fantasy, with Dietrich as the gypsy, the mystic, the mythical woman with a rich and mysterious past behind her. She never looked more beautiful and bewitching. Dietrich's daughter once asked Orson why he asked Marlene to play the part of a brothel madam. Welles smiled and said, "You never heard of typecasting?"

Happy with his work, Orson delivered Universal a rough cut of the film, under budget and within time. Welles was sure his career would now be back on track after a few missteps and clunkers, but then Universal took it from him, banned him from having any more involvement and re-edited it. Worse still, they went and put it on a double bill with another picture, ranked as a secondary B movie alongside the then higher profile, but now long forgotten, The Female Animal, which went out as the main presentation.

Though ignored at the time by audiences, it is now one of the prime examples of classic 1950s film noir, and remains an undisputed classic. Dietrich and Welles' moment together remains one of the finest of the fifties and one of the most iconic of Marlene's whole career, almost thirty years after she sang Falling in Love Again in The Blue Angel.

JUDGEMENT AT NURENBERG (1961)

Marlene Dietrich had her first role in the 1960s, at the age of sixty no less, in Stanley Kramer's Judgement at Nurenberg. It stars Spencer Tracy as Judge Dan Haywood as he is overseeing the trial of four men being accused of sadistic crimes during the Nazi reign in Germany. Burt Lancaster is Ernst Janning, an educated man who sentenced hundreds of people to their deaths, while Judy Garland, William Shatner and Montgomery Clift also have key roles.

Dietrich herself plays the widow of a German general who was sentenced to death by the allies, a role which though small is also a very important one, in that it explores the feelings and position of the spouse of a Nazi, from the viewpoint of someone personally close to the afflicter of the horror. Her scenes also provide a breather from the heavy courtroom scenes. Again, like in A Foreign Affair, this was close to home for Dietrich, and she was brave for taking on such sensitive material.

The film was a big success (making its budget back three times in the US alone), while it also attracted good reviews and awards, including a Best Actor Oscar for Maximillian Schell, who played the defence counsel. The New York Times called it "a powerful and persuasive film", while the New Yorker dubbed it a "bold and continuously exciting picture."

Few reviews at the time singled out Dietrich, but in retrospect, especially when looks at her development from The Blue Angel onwards, it's remarkable that a figure, once known primarily for her glamour and almost cartoonish sex appeal, could provide such subtleties to a powerful drama like this.

BLACK FOX: THE RISE AND FALL OF ADOLF HITLER
(1962)

Marlene Dietrich continued to explore the atrocities of the Nazis in 1962 when she agreed to narrate Louis Clyde Stoumen's documentary on Adolf Hitler, Black Fox. The film won the Best Documentary Feature Award at the Oscars, and was generally seen as an honourable and well executed biography of the 20th century's biggest monster. Even today, still widely available on DVD, it fails to be beaten. Of course, there have been countless films on Hitler since this one - some good, some bad - but there is a purity and directness (also a chilling element) to Stoumen's 90 minute exploration into this devil's life that makes it essential viewing. The fact it features the voice of the century's most loved German, Marlene Dietrich, a woman more qualified than any to voice this vitally important film, only adds to the authentic strength.

The music by Ezra Laderman is both beautiful and terrifying in equal measures, providing a fitting mood to accompany this often shocking footage. Dietrich's voice, as recognisable as can be, puts a poignant, sadly poetic slant on proceedings, and she does a better job, in her controlled manner, than any experienced narrator could have. The direction is superb, the various devices alluding Hitler to a force much darker than any man inspired and the pacing just right. Black Fox is highly recommended, though obviously remains upsetting viewing in parts.

PARIS WHEN IT SIZZLES (1964)

Richard Quine directed this long forgotten and far from worth remembering romantic comedy, starring the great Audrey Hepburn in one of her misguided ventures opposite William Holden. Noel Coward plays Alexander Myerheim, hiring screenwriting playboy Holden for a writing job, only to see him slack off until the very last minute when he plans to up his game and complete the script. Hepburn plays the secretary hired to type up the work, a woman who revitalises Holden's passion for life and with whom he, naturally, begins to fall in love.

Littered with star cameos, from Tony Curtis to Marlene Dietrich (who plays herself, clad in white, stepping out a flash white car in the film's brightest moment), it is utterly forgettable form start to finish, not to mention uninspired. Reviews were not kind. Variety called it "marshmallow-weight hokum", adding it was "contrived, preposterous and totally unmotivated". Quite what the filmmakers had in mind is anyone's guess, but this is a complete waste of time and money, the highlight in my humble opinion being Miss Dietrich's all too brief cameo.

JUST A GIGOLO (1979)

It took fifteen more years for Marlene Dietrich to be convinced to make another film appearance, and when she finally agreed to do it, for David Hemmings in his misguided David Bowie vehicle, Just a Gigolo, some people wondered why she had bothered. For some, it threatened to lessen her sizeable legacy, her intimidating myth. Others found her swan song fitting and poetic. One must remember that at this stage Dietrich was already living a reclusive life style in Paris. The rest of the film was to be set and filmed in Berlin, and when Marlene accepted the offer (for a large fee), she insisted her scenes be filmed separately in Paris. Naturally, the filmmakers complied.

Marlene's big moment comes when she sings, quietly I might add, the theme tune for the film. It's a sad, poignant moment, and by far the most worthwhile scene in the whole film. As her final moment on screen, it wasn't perfect, but it was certainly memorable.

Hemmings himself always said he was quite fond of the picture, while Bowie often expressed shame and embarrassment, seeing the whole debacle as a misfire. Bowie also said he did it as a favour to Hemmings and found the idea of being in a film with Marlene Dietrich (who he says was "dangled in front of him") too irresistible. It is certainly not a good film, though Hemmings was a decent director and did what he could with the limited material.

Rory MacLean was the assistant director on the film and later told The History Reader all about his first sighting of Dietrich, the enigmatic star, as she arrived on set. "At first the old woman who mounted the steps of the film studio brought back no memories of

Shanghai Express. She wore a tired denim suit and hid by the door. Her lips quivered as we were introduced to her. She refused to take off her dark glasses. The makeup artist moved to her side, and spirited her away into the dressing room. Two hours passed before she reappeared, wearing a wide brim hat and deep veil over her face. In costume she began to find her confidence, the clothes helping to ease her into the role. She walked onto the set without assistance, sat down and let her long skirt — split to the thigh — slip open. A woman of half her age would have been satisfied with those legs. As the crew tried not to stare, a smile fleeted across her face. As she would only sing once, we decided to run two cameras. I was asked to operate the second one. The lights were checked. Exposure and focus set. We took our positions, settled ourselves, waited for, 'Quiet please. Turn over. Sound rolling. Speed. Mark it. Scene 503 take 1. And action... I looked through the lens, and my eyes deceived me. There was no old woman standing before me. Instead the veil and a soft focus filter had transformed her. The key light caught her eyes and I saw the star of Blonde Venus and Touch of Evil, the legendary Dietrich."

MacLean's account certainly inspires awe, and the highlight of the whole thing is Dietrich's haunting scene. But reviews for the picture were savage. Bowie's performance (though to call it a performance is misguided) was torn to shreds, and the pop icon himself called it "my 32 Elvis movies rolled into one." Upon seeing the reactions, Hemmings pulled Just A Gigolo out of cinemas and re-cut the movie, though he could not save it from the dustbin of film history.

MARLENE (1984)

Now in her eighties, living a hermitic life style in her Paris apartment, and staying in bed and refusing to be seen by anyone but her daughter Maria Riva, Marlene was becoming strapped for cash. Making money by selling off old bits and pieces, and filling out interviews by hand for various papers, it was Maria who came up with the idea of taking part in a documentary on her life. Though Dietrich instantly dismissed the idea of being filmed (clearly, she did not want anyone to see the frail old woman she had become) she eventually agreed to make the film. At first she wanted Orson Welles, or even film historian and director Peter Bogdanovich, to piece it together, but in the end signed up to make it with actor and director Maximillian Schell, with whom she had worked on Judgement at Nuremberg. He was to record her voice only, and use film clips and news reels over the top. The plan was set.

Sadly the pair did not see eye to eye. When Schell turned up and told Dietrich he had been reading Proust in preparation for the interview, she thought him mad. But it was too late to reverse the decision and rip up the contract. Refusing to say much of any worth during their interview sessions, Schell constructed a film out of her stubbornness. It was a documentary like no other, and though Dietrich at first tried to have it withdrawn from circulation, once it was met with plaudits and acclaim she changed her mind and accepted it for what it was.

It may have been a nightmare experience for Schell and almost enough to give him a meltdown, but his suffering was worth it. Marlene, eventually released in 1984, is a compelling, compulsively engaging revelation, a glimpse into the mind and views of one of the 20th century's most beloved icons. There have been straight forward documentaries on Marlene of course, with talking head interviews with collaborators, film/news clips and extracts from TV chats with Marlene herself, but Schell's film is something else entirely, a totally individual experience where, though Dietrich as an old lady is never on screen, one almost feels like she is. Her voice, aged but still totally Dietrich in every way, becomes hypnotic, reflective as it is on the enigma of life, movies, fame and the illusion of immortality. A poignant and poetic film, it remains Dietrich's final say. Though her published memoirs have their fans, Maria Riva says there is little truth in the tome and only what Dietrich wanted the world to know. Marlene died in 1992, eight years after the documentary came out. Almost immediately, her daughter's book was released, which gave us both the woman behind the myth and the myth which often over took the woman. Maria's biography of her mother is essential of course, but there is a mystery and haunting quality to this documentary which, for me at least, makes it an incomparable experience, and perhaps the most revealing and rewarding trip into the folkloric world of Marlene Dietrich.

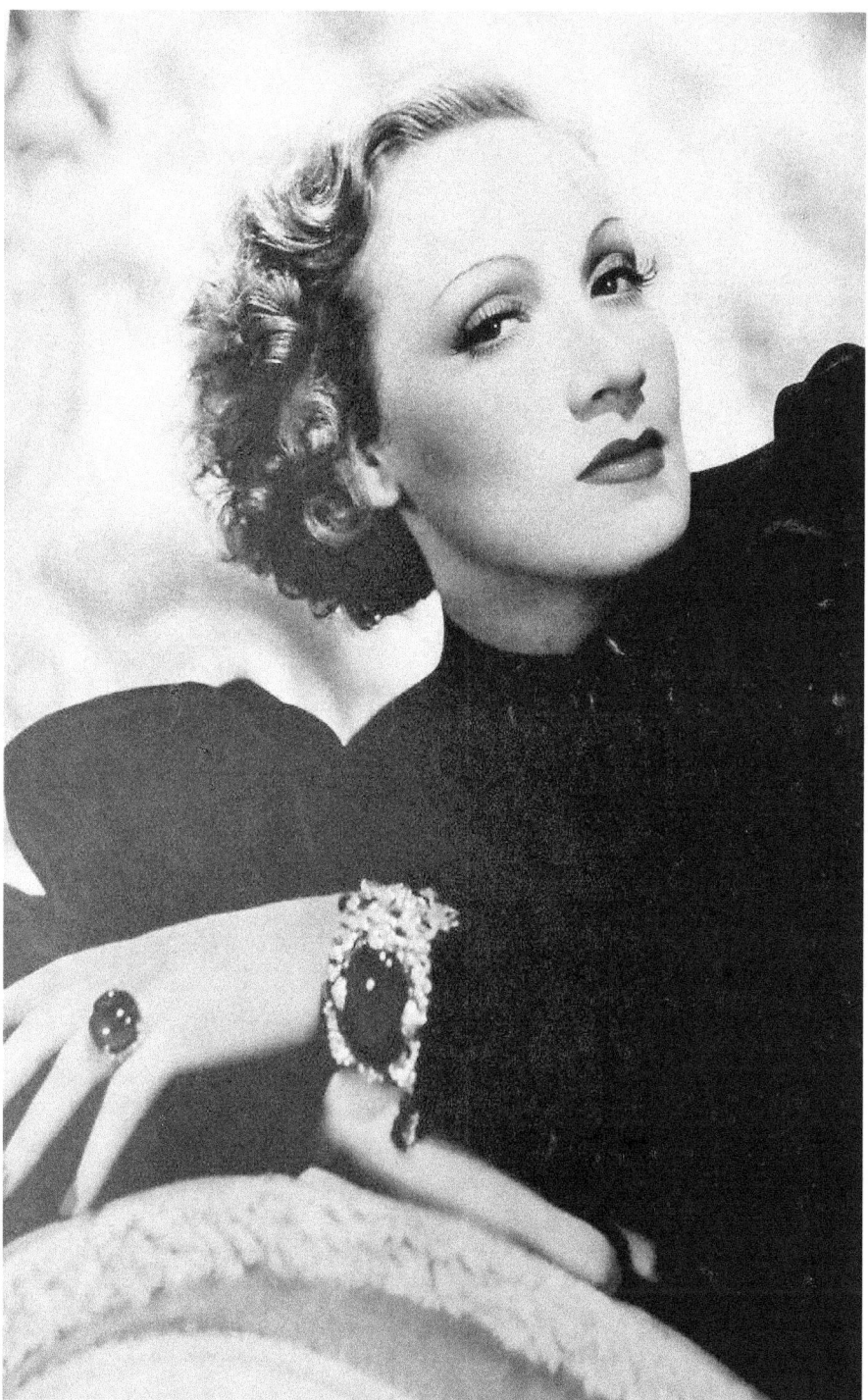

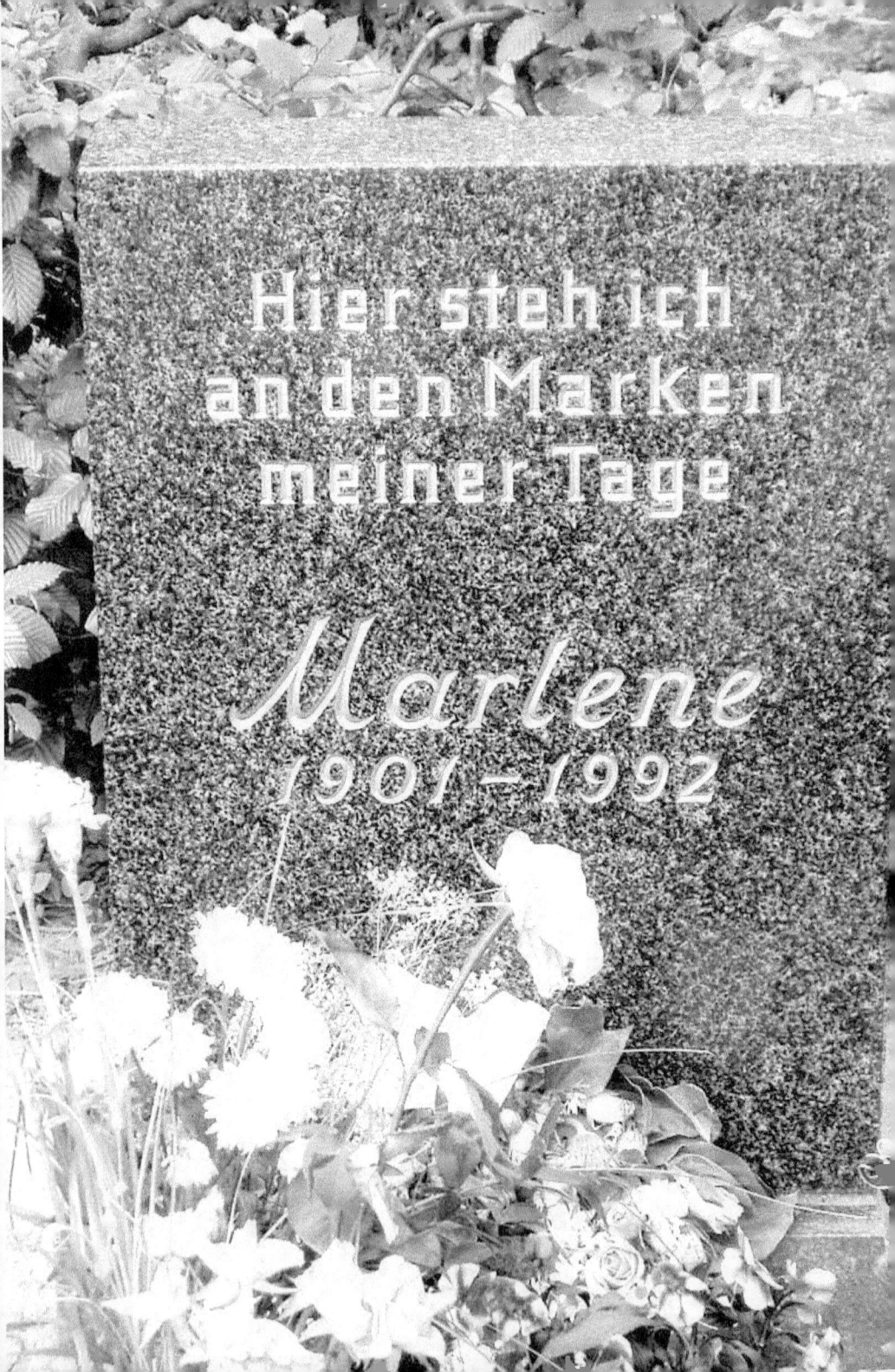

References

The following books were useful in completion of this book;

Marlene Dietrich, by Maria Riva

The Films of Marlene Dietrich, by Homer Dickens

Dietrich, by Alexander Walker

Marlene Dietrich: Life and Legend, by Stephen Bach

Marlene Dietrich: Photographs and Memories

Marlene: A Personal Biography, by Charlotte Chandler

My Life, by Marlene Dietrich

Articles form these publications and websites;

Variety

New York Times

The Times

The Observer

Empire Magazine

All pictures in this book have been taken from the public domain archives and Commons.

ABOUT CHRIS WADE

Chris Wade is a UK based writer, filmmaker and musician. As well as running the acclaimed music project Dodson and Fogg, he has written books on The Kinks, Malcolm McDowell, Captain Beefheart, Robert De Niro and many others. He has also released audiobooks of his comedic fiction, such as Cutey and the Sofaguard, narrated by Rik Mayall. His other projects include Hound Dawg Magazine, for which he has interviewed such people as Sharon Stone, Donovan and Jethro Tull's Ian Anderson. His art films include The Apple Picker (winning Best Film at the Sydney World Film Festival, and featuring Toyah Willcox and Nigel Planer), and he's made documentaries on George Melly, Lindsay Anderson, Charlie Chaplin and Orson Welles.

More info at his website: wisdomtwinsbooks.weebly.com

www.ingramcontent.com/pod-product-compliance
Lightning Source LLC
Chambersburg PA
CBHW071437180526
45170CB00001B/372